BELIZE
A POCKET TRAVEL
GUIDE 2024

Your Updated and Comprehensive travel
Companion for exploring the top attractions
and hidden gems of Belize

JAMES D. FLICK

BELIZE MAP

TABLE OF CONTENT

INTRODUCTION

As the plane descended through the clouds, the azure expanse of the Caribbean Sea unfolded beneath me, its crystalline waters reflecting the vibrant hues of the sky. Anticipation fluttered within me, a symphony of excitement and curiosity, as Belize, a land steeped in ancient Maya mysteries and adorned with emerald rainforests, beckoned me closer.

The plane touched down, its wheels humming against the tarmac of Philip S.W. Goldson International Airport. Stepping onto Belizean soil, I was immediately enveloped by a symphony of sounds – the rhythmic sway of reggae beats, the chatter of Creole, a language as vibrant as the people it served, and the distant calls of exotic birds echoing from the depths of the rainforest.

A balmy breeze caressed my skin, carrying with it the tantalizing aromas of Belizean cuisine – spicy stews, fresh seafood, and the sweet allure of local fruits. The air was alive with energy, a palpable blend of ancient traditions and modern exuberance.

As I ventured into the heart of Belize City, a kaleidoscope of colors exploded before me – brightly painted buildings adorned with intricate Mayan motifs, bustling markets overflowing with fresh produce and handcrafted souvenirs, and lively streets pulsating with the rhythm of Belizean life.

The allure of Belize extended far beyond its captivating cities. A tapestry of natural wonders awaited, each more mesmerizing than the last. Pristine beaches fringed with swaying palm trees, their sands as soft as velvet, beckoned me to sun-kissed shores. Lush rainforests, teeming with exotic flora and fauna, whispered tales of ancient civilizations that once thrived amidst their emerald embrace.

Belize, a land where time seemed to slow, where the rhythm of life flowed to the beat of the Caribbean Sea, beckoned me to embark on an unforgettable odyssey. With each step, each encounter, I felt a connection to a place that defied definition, a land where magic and reality intertwined, where the spirit of adventure soared as high as the ancient temples that stood as silent sentinels of a forgotten past.

So, dear traveler, embark on this journey with me, as we delve into the heart of Belize, a place where enchantment awaits, and unforgettable memories are waiting to be made. Let the magic of Belize transport you to a realm where adventure and serenity intertwine, where ancient wonders and vibrant cultures collide, and where the beauty of nature will forever captivate your heart.

Why Visit Belize?

Belize, a hidden gem nestled in the heart of Central America, offers an abundance of reasons to visit. Whether you're seeking adventure, relaxation, cultural immersion, or a unique blend of all three, Belize has something to captivate every traveler.

Explore Ancient Mayan Ruins

Belize is home to some of the most impressive ancient Mayan ruins in the world, offering a glimpse into the fascinating history of this once-powerful civilization. Wander through the towering temples of Caracol, the largest ancient Maya city in Belize, or climb the pyramids of Xunantunich, overlooking the lush rainforest. Imagine the lives of the Maya as you explore their intricate carvings, ball courts, and plazas, and gain a deeper understanding of their rich culture.

Vibrant Culture

Belize's culture is a vibrant tapestry woven from diverse influences, reflecting its rich history and multicultural population. Experience the Garifuna culture, known for its lively music, delicious cuisine, and colorful clothing. Immerse yourself in the Creole culture, a blend of European, African, and Caribbean influences, evident in the language, music, and cuisine. Discover the Mennonite communities, known for their traditional lifestyle and craftsmanship.

Belize Barrier Reef

Belize is home to the world's second-largest barrier reef, a UNESCO World Heritage Site and a haven for marine life. Snorkel or dive among vibrant coral reefs teeming with colorful fish, turtles, and sharks. Explore the Belize Blue Hole, a natural wonder with a depth of over 400 feet, or discover the underwater caves of the Belize Barrier Reef Reserve System.

Thrill of Adventure

Belize is an adventurer's paradise, offering a variety of adrenaline-pumping activities. Go cave tubing through subterranean rivers, rappel down waterfalls, or soar through the jungle canopy on a zipline adventure. Embark on a jungle trek, discovering hidden waterfalls, ancient Mayan sites, and exotic wildlife. Experience the thrill of kayaking or stand-up paddleboarding along the idyllic coastline.

Pristine Beaches

Belize's coastline is dotted with pristine beaches, offering the perfect escape for relaxation and rejuvenation. Lounge on the soft white sand, soak up the sun, and take a refreshing dip in the crystal-clear waters of the Caribbean Sea. Explore the charming coastal towns and villages, where you'll find friendly locals, delicious seafood, and a laid-back atmosphere.

Connect with Nature

Belize is a haven for nature lovers, with lush rainforests, diverse wildlife, and a variety of ecosystems to explore. Hike through the verdant jungles of the Cockscomb Basin Wildlife Sanctuary, home to the endangered scarlet macaw. Spot exotic birds, monkeys, and other wildlife in the Belize Zoo, a conservation organization dedicated to protecting Belize's native species. Explore the fascinating ecosystems of the Belize Barrier Reef Reserve System, including mangroves, seagrass beds, and lagoons.

Authentic Cuisine

Belize's cuisine is a reflection of its diverse cultural influences, offering a unique blend of flavors. Savor the taste of fresh seafood, including lobster, conch, and snapper, prepared in traditional Belizean dishes. Sample the fiery flavors of Garifuna cuisine, known for its use of coconut milk and spices. Enjoy the hearty Creole dishes, a fusion of European, African, and Caribbean influences.

Discover Hidden Gems

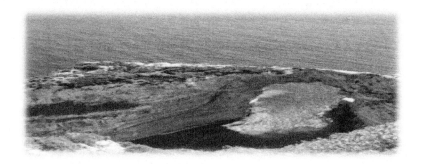

Belize is home to a wealth of hidden gems waiting to be discovered. Explore the secluded beaches of Caye Caulker, a car-free island known for its relaxed atmosphere and excellent snorkeling. Hike to the top of Victoria Peak, the highest point in Belize, for breathtaking panoramic views of the surrounding countryside. Discover the ancient Mayan ruins of Nim Li Punit, nestled in the depths of the jungle.

explore the Belizean Way of Life

Belize is known for its friendly and welcoming people, who are proud of their country's rich culture and natural beauty. Immerse yourself in the Belizean way of life, characterized by a laid-back attitude, a strong sense of community, and a deep respect for the environment. Experience the warmth and hospitality of the Belizean people, who are always eager to share their stories and traditions.

Unforgettable Memories

Belize is a country that leaves an indelible mark on the hearts of its visitors. With its natural wonders, cultural heritage, and endless opportunities for adventure, Belize offers an unforgettable travel experience that will stay with you long after you've left its shores. Create memories that will last a lifetime as you explore the diverse landscapes, immerse yourself in the vibrant culture, and connect with the warm and welcoming people of Belize.

Geographical Overview

Belize, nestled along the Caribbean coast of Central America, is a land of captivating beauty and diverse landscapes. Its territory encompasses 22,966 square kilometers (8,867 square miles), stretching from the lush rainforests of the Maya Mountains in the southwest to the pristine beaches and coral reefs of the Caribbean Sea in the east.

Key Geographical Features

1. Coastal Plains: Belize's coastline stretches along the Caribbean Sea for 386 kilometers (240 miles), boasting pristine beaches, lagoons, and offshore islands.

2. Maya Mountains: Located in the southwest, the Maya Mountains rise to an elevation of 1,124 meters (3,689 feet) at Victoria Peak, the highest point in Belize. These mountains are home to diverse ecosystems, including rainforests, waterfalls, and caves.

3. Belize Barrier Reef: The world's second-largest barrier reef system, the Belize Barrier Reef stretches for 300 kilometers (186 miles) along the Belizean coast. This UNESCO World Heritage Site is a haven for marine life, with over 500 species of fish, 70 species of coral, and countless other marine organisms.

4. Lowlands and River Valleys: The northern and central regions of Belize are characterized by low-lying plains and river valleys, home to lush rainforests, agricultural lands, and scattered settlements.

5. Cayes and Islands: Dotting the Caribbean Sea off the coast of Belize are numerous cayes and islands, offering idyllic retreats for relaxation and exploration. These islands are popular for snorkeling, diving, and fishing.

Climate and Biodiversity

Belize enjoys a tropical savanna climate, with warm temperatures throughout the year and distinct wet and dry seasons. The rainy season runs from May to November, while the dry season spans from December to April. Belize's diverse ecosystems support a rich biodiversity, with over 5,000 species of plants, 600 species of birds, and 60 species of mammals.

Cultural Diversity

Belize is a multicultural nation, home to a diverse array of ethnic groups, each contributing to its vibrant cultural tapestry. These groups have enriched Belize's society with their unique traditions, languages, cuisines, and artistic expressions.

Ethnic Groups

Belize's major ethnic groups include:

1. Mestizo: The Mestizo people, constituting around 50% of the population, descend from Spanish and Maya ancestry. They represent the largest ethnic group in Belize.

2. Creole: The Creole people, accounting for approximately 25% of the population, are descendants of African and European ancestry. Their culture is evident in the Belize Kriol language, punta music, and Creole cuisine.

3. Maya: The Maya people, comprising around 11% of the population, are the indigenous inhabitants of Belize. They have preserved their distinct culture, language, and traditions, including ancient Mayan ruins and artifacts.

4. Garifuna: The Garifuna people, making up about 6% of the population, are descendants of West African people who were exiled to the Caribbean. Their culture is characterized by lively punta music, colorful clothing, and delicious cuisine.

5. Other Groups: Belize also hosts smaller populations of Mennonites, East Indians, Chinese, Lebanese, and Europeans, each contributing to the country's cultural diversity.

Cultural Influences

Belize's cultural landscape is shaped by a blend of influences, including:

1. Maya Heritage: The ancient Maya civilization left an indelible mark on Belize, with remnants of their cities, temples, and artifacts still present. Their influence is evident in traditional practices, language, and cuisine.

2. European Colonization: Spanish and British colonization brought European languages, traditions, and religious practices to Belize. These influences are interwoven with the country's cultural fabric.

3. African Heritage: The arrival of enslaved Africans contributed significantly to Belize's culture, particularly in the development of Creole language, punta music, and culinary traditions.

4. Garifuna Culture: The Garifuna people's arrival in the 19th century enriched Belize's cultural diversity with their lively music, colorful clothing, and unique cuisine.

Cultural Significance

Cultural diversity is a defining characteristic of Belize, playing a crucial role in shaping its national identity and attracting tourism. Visitors can immerse themselves in Belize's rich culture through its festivals, cuisine, music, traditional crafts, and interactions with the diverse communities that call Belize home.

History and Heritage

Belize's history is a captivating narrative intertwined with ancient civilizations, colonial powers, cultural diversity, and the struggle for independence. From its early Maya inhabitants to its current status as a sovereign nation, Belize's heritage is a testament to its resilience and cultural richness.

Maya Legacy

The ancient Maya civilization flourished in Belize from around 2500 BC to 900 AD, leaving behind an impressive legacy of temples, cities, and artifacts. Belize boasts some of the most significant Maya sites in the region, including Caracol, the largest ancient Maya city in Belize, and Xunantunich, a magnificent temple complex overlooking the Belize River.

Colonial Era

In the 16th century, Spanish explorers arrived in Belize, establishing a presence along the coast. However, due to fierce resistance from the Maya and the harsh terrain, the Spanish never fully controlled the territory. In the 17th century, English settlers began arriving in Belize, attracted by the abundance of logwood, a valuable dye used in textile production. These settlers established small settlements along the coast, which gradually grew into trading centers.

Struggle for Independence

During the 18th and 19th centuries, Belize remained a British colony, despite repeated attempts by Spain to claim the territory. The Belizean people, a mix of Maya, European, and African descendants, developed a distinct Creole culture and a strong sense of self-determination. Throughout the 20th century, Belizeans campaigned for independence from Britain, facing challenges such as Guatemala's territorial claims and economic pressures.

Gaining Independence

On September 21, 1981, Belize finally achieved independence after over 300 years of British rule. The newfound independence marked a significant milestone in Belize's history, allowing the country to chart its own course and celebrate its unique cultural identity.

Cultural Heritage

Belize's cultural heritage is a blend of Maya, European, African, and Garifuna influences. This diversity is reflected in the country's language, music, cuisine, and traditions. Belize Kriol, a Creole language based on English, is widely spoken alongside English and Spanish. Lively punta music, with its African roots, fills the air during festivals and celebrations. Belizean cuisine is a fusion of flavors, from spicy Garifuna dishes to hearty Creole meals.

Historical Sites and Landmarks

Belize is dotted with historical sites and landmarks that offer glimpses into its rich past. Ancient Maya ruins, such as Caracol and Xunantunich, stand as testaments to the region's once-powerful civilization. Colonial-era towns, like Belize City and Dangriga, preserve remnants of British architecture and heritage. Museums and cultural centers provide insights into Belize's diverse history and cultural traditions.

Preserving Heritage

The preservation of Belize's historical and cultural heritage is a vital undertaking, ensuring that these legacies are passed down to future generations. Organizations like the Institute of Archaeology and the National Institute of Culture and History play a crucial role in protecting and promoting Belize's cultural heritage.

Heritage Tourism

Heritage tourism plays a significant role in Belize's economy, attracting visitors interested in exploring the country's rich history and diverse cultures. Heritage sites, museums, and cultural events offer unique experiences that immerse visitors in Belize's past and present.

Belize's history and heritage are integral to its national identity and a source of pride for its people. By preserving and celebrating its heritage, Belize continues to captivate visitors from around the world, offering a glimpse into its captivating past and vibrant cultural tapestry.

weather and best time to visit

Belize experiences two distinct seasons: the dry season (November to April) and the rainy season (May to October). The dry season is generally considered the best time to visit Belize, as the weather is warm and sunny with low humidity. However, the rainy season can also be a good time to visit, as the crowds are smaller and the rain typically falls in short bursts, leaving plenty of time for sunshine and outdoor activities.

Dry Season (November to April)

- Temperatures: Average temperatures range from the mid-70s to mid-80s Fahrenheit (24-29°C).
- Precipitation: Low rainfall, with occasional showers or thunderstorms.
- Humidity: Lower humidity levels compared to the rainy season.

Rainy Season (May to October)

- Temperatures: Average temperatures remain similar to the dry season, with occasional hotter days.
- Precipitation: Increased rainfall, with frequent showers and thunderstorms.
- Humidity: Higher humidity levels, especially during the peak rainy months (June to September).

Best Time to Visit

The best time to visit Belize depends on your preferences for weather and crowds. If you prefer warm, sunny weather with low humidity, then the dry season is the best time to visit. However, if you don't mind a bit of rain and don't mind crowds, then the rainy season can also be a good time to visit.

Here is a more detailed breakdown of the best time to visit Belize for specific activities:

- Beaches and snorkeling: The best time for beaches and snorkeling is during the dry season, as the water is clearer and the seas are calmer.
- Diving: Diving is good all year round, but the best visibility is during the dry season.
- Hiking and jungle treks: Hiking and jungle treks are good all year round, but the trails can be muddy during the rainy season.
- Birding: Birding is good all year round, but the best time to see migrating birds is during the spring and fall.
- Cultural events: There are many cultural events throughout the year, but the most popular ones are held during the dry season.

Here are some additional things to keep in mind when planning your trip to Belize:

- The peak tourist season in Belize is from December to April. If you want to avoid crowds, consider visiting during the shoulder seasons (May to June or September to October).
- The cost of travel and accommodation in Belize is generally higher during the peak season. If you're on a budget, consider visiting during the shoulder seasons or rainy season.

- Belize is a hurricane-prone country. The hurricane season runs from June to November. If you're planning to visit during this time, be sure to purchase travel insurance that covers trip cancellation and interruption.

budgeting for your trip

Accommodation:

- Budget: $30-$50 per night for a hostel or guesthouse
- Mid-range: $50-$100 per night for a hotel or condo
- Luxury: $100+ per night for a resort or villa

Food:

- Budget: $10-$20 per day for meals at local restaurants and street vendors

- Mid-range: $20-$40 per day for meals at mid-range restaurants
- Luxury: $40+ per day for meals at upscale restaurants

Transportation:

- Budget: $5-$10 per day for local buses and taxis
- Mid-range: $10-$20 per day for car rentals or private transfers
- Luxury: $20+ per day for private transportation and tours

Activities:

- Budget: $5-$10 per day for free activities like hiking, swimming, and exploring ruins
- Mid-range: $10-$20 per day for paid activities like snorkeling, diving, and ziplining
- Luxury: $20+ per day for private excursions and guided tours

Other expenses:

- Souvenirs: $10-$20 per day
- Alcohol: $5-$10 per day
- Tipping: 10-15% of total bill

Total:

- Budget: $50-$100 per day
- Mid-range: $100-$200 per day
- Luxury: $200+ per day

Please note that this is just a sample budget, and your actual expenses will vary depending on your travel style and preferences.

Be sure to factor in the cost of your flights, travel insurance, and any other additional expenses you may have.

Here are some additional tips for saving money on your trip to Belize:

- Book your flights and accommodation in advance, especially during the peak season.
- Consider traveling during the shoulder seasons (May to June or September to October) when prices are lower.
- Stay in hostels or guesthouses to save on accommodation costs.
- Eat at local restaurants and street vendors to save on food costs.
- Take advantage of free activities like hiking, swimming, and exploring ruins.
- Purchase a Belize Tourism Board Pass to save on the cost of activities and attractions.
- Consider renting a car for a few days to save on transportation costs.
- Bring your own snorkel gear to save on rental fees.
- Pack light to avoid baggage fees.
- Drink tap water instead of bottled water.
- Take advantage of happy hours and drink specials.
- Ask for discounts and negotiate prices when shopping at local markets

Visa Requirements

Belize offers a relatively straightforward visa application process for most nationalities, allowing visitors to enjoy its vibrant culture, stunning natural beauty, and diverse adventures. Here's a comprehensive guide to visa and entry requirements for Belize:

Visa Exemption:

Most nationals from developed countries, including the United States, Canada, the United Kingdom, Australia, and most European Union member states, are eligible to enter Belize without a visa for up to 30 days for tourism or business purposes.

Visa Requirements:

If you are a citizen of a country that requires a visa to enter Belize, you should apply for a visa at the nearest Belizean embassy or consulate. The visa application process typically involves submitting a completed visa application form, providing supporting documents such as a valid passport, passport-size photo, proof of travel arrangements, and proof of financial means, and paying the applicable visa fee.

Tourist Visa:

A tourist visa is the most common type of visa for visitors to Belize. It allows you to stay in Belize for up to 30 days for tourism purposes.

Business Visa:

A business visa is required if you intend to engage in business activities in Belize, such as attending meetings, conferences, or seminars. It allows you to stay in Belize for up to 90 days for business purposes.

Visa Extensions:

If you wish to extend your stay in Belize beyond the initial authorized period, you must apply for a visa extension at the Department of

Immigration in Belize City. Visa extensions are typically granted for additional 30-day periods.

Entry Requirements

Upon arrival in Belize, you will be required to present a valid passport with at least six months of validity remaining, a completed immigration form, and proof of onward travel or return ticket. You may also be asked to provide proof of financial means and accommodation.

Departure Tax:

A departure tax of approximately BZ$50 (approximately US$25) is applied to all passengers leaving Belize on international flights. This fee is typically included in the airline ticket price.

Additional Considerations:

- Ensure your passport is in good condition and has at least six months of validity remaining beyond your planned departure date from Belize.

- Inquire about any particular luggage rules or limitations from your airline.

- Be prepared to provide proof of onward travel or return ticket upon arrival in Belize.

- Keep your travel documents, including passport, visa, and travel insurance documents, secure throughout your trip.

- Familiarize yourself with Belize's currency, exchange rates, and tipping etiquette.

- Respect local customs and traditions.

- When visiting places of worship or cultural attractions, dress modestly.

- Bargain respectfully when shopping at local markets.

- Avoid public displays of wealth or expensive jewelry.

By following these visa and entry requirements, you can ensure a smooth and hassle-free travel experience in Belize, allowing you to fully immerse yourself in its vibrant culture and natural splendor.

Getting there

By Air:

Belize is served by two international airports:

- Philip S. W. Goldson International Airport (BZE), located near Belize City, is the main gateway to the country. It is served by a variety of airlines, including American Airlines, Delta Air Lines, United Airlines, and Southwest Airlines.

- Hector Silva Airstrip (TZA), located on Ambergris Caye, is a smaller airport that serves the islands of Ambergris Caye and Caye Caulker. It is served by a few smaller airlines, including Maya Island Air and Tropic Air.

By Land:

Belize can also be reached by land from Guatemala and Mexico. There are several border crossings, including:

- Benque Viejo del Carmen-Melchor de Mencos border crossing: This crossing is located near Benque Viejo del Carmen in Belize and Melchor de Mencos in Guatemala. It is the most popular crossing between the two countries.

- Chetumal-Belize City border crossing: This crossing is located near Chetumal in Mexico and Belize City in Belize. It is a longer drive than the Benque Viejo crossing, but it is a good option if you are coming from Mexico City or the Yucatán Peninsula.

By Sea:

Belize can also be reached by sea from Guatemala and Honduras. There are several ferry services, including:

- Belize Water Taxi: This ferry service operates between Belize City and Puerto Cortés, Honduras.

- San Pedro Belize Express: This ferry service operates between Belize City and San Pedro Sula, Honduras.

- West End Ferry: This ferry service operates between Belize City and West End, Roatán, Honduras.

Once you arrive in Belize, you can get around by taxi, bus, rental car, or boat. Taxis are readily available in all major towns and cities. Buses are a good option for traveling between towns and cities, but they can be slow and crowded. Rental cars are a good option if you want to explore the country at your own pace, but they can be expensive. Boats are the best way to get around the islands and cays.

Currency and Banking

Currency: The official currency of Belize is the Belize Dollar (BZD), which is pegged to the United States Dollar (USD) at a rate of 2 BZD to 1 USD. US dollars are widely accepted throughout Belize, often at a 2:1 exchange rate. However, using Belizean dollars is recommended for smaller transactions and to avoid carrying large amounts of US currency.

ATMs: ATMs are readily available in Belize's major cities, towns, and tourist destinations. Most ATMs accept international credit and debit cards with the Cirrus, Maestro, or Plus logos. Be sure to inform your bank of your travel plans to avoid transaction declines.

Banks: Belize has several commercial banks, including Belize Bank, Atlantic Bank, and First Caribbean International Bank. Banks typically operate during regular business hours, Monday to Friday.

Exchange Rates: Currency exchange services are available at banks, hotels, and some tourist shops. Exchange rates may vary slightly between locations.

Credit Cards: Major credit cards such as Visa, Mastercard, and American Express are widely accepted in Belize, particularly in larger establishments and tourist areas. Smaller businesses and vendors may prefer cash payments.

Traveler's Checks: Traveler's checks are less common in Belize, but they can be exchanged at banks and some hotels. It's advisable to convert them to Belizean dollars for convenience.

Tipping: Tipping is customary in Belize, with a standard tip of 10-15% for good service. Tipping is appreciated for services such as taxis, restaurants, hotel staff, and tour guides.

Taxes: Belize's Goods and Services Tax (GST) is 12.5%, which is added to most consumer goods and services. A departure tax of approximately BZ$50 (approximately US$25) is applied to passengers leaving the country on international flights.

Hotels and Resorts

Victoria House Resort & Spa

The magnificent Victoria House Resort & Spa is the height of luxury, tucked away in the center of Ambergris Caye, Belize. This tranquil hideaway, which has earned a five-star rating, provides a unique experience on the immaculate beaches of the Caribbean Sea.

Upon arrival, visitors are greeted with unmatched hospitality. A flawless check-in is ensured by the kind and accommodating personnel, laying the groundwork for an enjoyable stay. The resort's tastefully furnished rooms and suites, complete with contemporary conveniences and breathtaking views of the garden or the sea, exude calm and sophistication.

Victoria House meets all demands, whether it a family getaway or a romantic retreat. Savor delectable meals prepared with regional ingredients in the restaurant's award-winning kitchen, or revitalize yourself in the spa with opulent treatments that soothe the mind and body.

Set out on customized excursions handpicked by the concierge, discovering the mysteries of the Belize Barrier Reef or ancient Mayan ruins. An amazing stay is guaranteed at Victoria House Resort & Spa, where each visitor will get a personalized experience.

Starting at around $350 per night (estimate only; subject to seasonal variations and room preference).

Coco Beach Resort

Discover the allure of Coco Beach Resort, a charming four-star hideaway tucked away amid the breathtaking shoreline of Ambergris Caye in Belize. This resort, which embodies luxury with a laid-back feel, provides the ideal fusion of contemporary comforts and Caribbean appeal.

Welcomed by soothing seaside breezes, visitors find a warm and friendly environment from the minute they set foot on the resort grounds. Vibrant Belizean accents decorate the spacious suites and villas, which provide comfort and elegance along with private balconies or terraces that look out over lush gardens or crystal-clear waterways.

Enjoy a variety of activities at Coco Beach, such as relaxing by the pools, eating on the beach, or getting spa services. Due to the resort's commitment to providing individualized service, all visitors' demands are satisfied.

While those seeking tranquility may repose on the immaculate beach or partake in the resort's specially designed activities, adventurers can take use of the resort as a starting point for exhilarating water sports and reef excursions, making for an unforgettable stay.

Starting at $250 per night (estimate only; subject to seasonal variations and room preference).

Eco-Lodges and Jungle Resorts

Chan Chich Lodge

Nestled in the middle of Belize's pristine jungle, among the ancient Mayan ruins, Chan Chich Lodge is a haven for explorers and nature lovers. This five-star resort provides an experience that cannot be found anywhere else in the middle of the forest.

The sound of tropical birdsongs and verdant foliage greets visitors to this private nature reserve. The lodge offers the ideal balance of luxury and natural immersion with its tastefully rustic but beautiful rooms and cabanas that provide breath-taking views of the surrounding environment.

At Chan Chich Lodge, there are many opportunities for exploration and adventure, ranging from thrilling walks through the forest paths to guided tours of the ancient Mayan ruins. Savor regional specialties made with fresh ingredients, indulge in farm-to-table dining, or just unwind by the pool while taking in the views and sounds of the rainforest.

Starting at around $450 per night (estimate only; subject to seasonal variations and room preference).

Black Rock Lodge

Nestled along the banks of the Macal River, Black Rock Lodge is a four-star eco-lodge where you can immerse yourself in the natural beauties of Belize. This resort, surrounded by towering cliffs and lush jungles, provides an alluring haven for environmentally concerned tourists looking for something special.

The peaceful atmosphere and kind greetings of the lodge welcome visitors as they enter. Modern amenities blended with rustic charm among breathtaking views of the river and forest, the lodge's riverside cottages and treehouses provide a quiet haven for travelers.

There are many of outdoor activities at Black Rock Lodge. Visitors may take kayaks or inner tubes down the river, go on guided treks, or go birding. Savor substantial meals in the lodge's restaurant, which serves genuine Belizean cuisine and uses ingredients that are acquired locally, after an exciting day of exploring.

Starting at $200 per night (estimate only; subject to seasonal variations and room preference).

Pook's Hill Lodge

Tucked away in a secluded jungle reserve, Pook's Hill Lodge offers guests a quiet haven among the breathtaking scenery of Belize. This four-star eco-lodge provides a peaceful haven for those looking to unwind and take in the abundance of wildlife in the nation.

Entranced by quaint thatched-roof cabanas, visitors are surrounded by luxuriant tropical vegetation and animals. All of the accommodations provide a comfortable haven to retreat to after a day of exploring, combining contemporary conveniences with rustic charm.

A portal to adventure, Pook's Hill Lodge offers access to neighboring Mayan sites, cave expeditions, and animal encounters. The lodge's grounds have natural paths that guests may explore, as well as a welcoming pool where they can unwind and take in the peace and beauty of the rainforest.

Pricing: Approximate starting price each night is $180, subject on seasonal variations and room choices.

Guesthouses and Bed and Breakfasts

Bella's Backpackers Hostel

Bella's Backpackers Hostel, tucked away in the center of Belize, provides tourists on a tight budget with a lively and sociable base for seeing the beauties of the nation. This hostel offers a pleasant and reasonably priced stay with an emphasis on community and a warm environment.

A cozy and welcoming atmosphere greets visitors as soon as they enter. The vibrantly decorated private rooms and dorms at the hostel provide a cozy place to rest after a day of exploration.

At Bella's, friendship blossoms as guests make meals together in the shared kitchen, engage in group activities, and exchange tales in the common areas. The hostel's strategic position makes it simple to visit neighboring sites and engage in local activities.

Pricing: Approximate estimates, depending to seasonal variations and room choices, start at $20 per night for dorms and $50 per night for private rooms.

Venus Hotel

At the Venus Hotel, an urban haven in a prominent location in Belize, experience contemporary luxury and convenience. Sophisticated and practical, this three-star hotel provides a chic stay for both leisure and business guests.

Upon arrival, visitors are greeted with a chic and modern environment. Sleek furnishings, luxurious bedding, and contemporary conveniences in the hotel's well-appointed rooms and suites provide a peaceful stay in the middle of the busy city.

The Venus Hotel is the perfect place to unwind after a long day of sightseeing or business meetings. Visitors may take advantage of the hotel's handy position for neighboring attractions and city amenities, relax in the lounge areas, and savor delectable meals at the on-site restaurant.

Pricing: Approximate estimates, depending to seasonal variations and room selection, start at $90 per night for regular rooms and $150 per night for suites.

Amber Sunset Jungle Resort

Travelers seeking peace and the embrace of nature are invited to Amber Sunset rainforest Resort, which is tucked away in Belize's verdant rainforest. Offering a peaceful environment and an emphasis on environmentally conscious lodging, this four-star resort provides a haven from everyday life.

As they arrive, guests are welcomed by the sounds of nature and shown into quaint jungle huts furnished with contemporary conveniences and a touch of rustic elegance. Every lodging provides stunning views of the forest that surrounds it, creating a tranquil haven for getting back in touch with the natural world.

Guests may rest by the pool, stroll along nature paths at their own pace, or just unwind while listening to the sounds of the jungle thanks to the resort's peaceful atmosphere. The resort provides unique nature-based experiences and arranges guided visits to neighboring destinations for adventure lovers.

Remember that prices can fluctuate based on factors like the time of year, room type, and availability. It's always a good idea to book accommodations well in advance, especially during the peak tourist season in Belize, which is typically from December to April.

Transportation options

Domestic Flights

Belize offers a convenient and efficient domestic air transportation system, connecting major towns, cities, and islands within the country. Two main airlines operate domestic flights in Belize: Tropic Air and Maya Island Air.

Tropic Air:

Tropic Air, Belize's oldest airline, offers a comprehensive network of domestic flights, including:

- From Belize City (BZE) to San Pedro (SPR), Ambergris Caye

- From Belize City (BZE) to Caye Caulker (CUK)

- From Belize City (BZE) to Dangriga (DGA)

- From Belize City (BZE) to Hopkins (HOP)

- From Belize City (BZE) to Placencia (PLJ)

Maya Island Air:

Maya Island Air, another major domestic airline, provides flights to:

- From Belize City (BZE) to San Pedro (SPR), Ambergris Caye

- From Belize City (BZE) to Caye Caulker (CUK)

- From Belize City (BZE) to Corozal (CZH)

- From Belize City (BZE) to Dangriga (DGA)

- From Belize City (BZE) to Orange Walk (ORZ)

Booking Domestic Flights:

Domestic flights in Belize can be booked directly through the airlines' websites, travel agencies, or hotel concierge desks. Advance booking is recommended, especially during peak season, to secure desired flight schedules and seating.

Domestic Airport Fees:

Departing passengers from domestic flights within Belize are subject to a departure tax of approximately BZ$50 (approximately US$25).

Luggage Allowance:

Domestic airlines typically allow one checked bag weighing up to 50 lbs (23 kg) and one carry-on bag weighing up to 10 lbs (4.5 kg). Additional baggage fees may apply for exceeding the allowance.

Travel Documents:

For domestic flights within Belize, passengers only need to present a valid government-issued photo ID.

Scheduled Flight Times:

Domestic flights operate on regular schedules, with multiple daily flights between major destinations. Flight times are generally short, ranging from 15 minutes to 45 minutes.

Charter Flights:

In addition to scheduled flights, charter options are also available for private or group travel to various destinations within Belize. Charter flights offer flexibility in scheduling and itinerary planning.

Luggage Storage:

Most domestic airports in Belize offer luggage storage facilities for passengers who wish to explore the area before or after their flights.

Ground Transportation:

Upon arrival at domestic airports, passengers can easily access ground transportation options such as taxis, rental cars, shuttles, or public buses.

Utilizing domestic air transportation in Belize provides a convenient and efficient way to explore the country's diverse destinations, from bustling cities to secluded islands, offering a seamless travel experience.

Buses and Coaches

Buses and coaches play a vital role in Belize's public transportation system, providing affordable and accessible connections between major towns, cities, and villages throughout the country. Whether you're seeking a budget-friendly option or a comfortable journey, Belize's bus and coach services offer a range of choices to suit your travel needs.

Local Bus Services:

Belize's local bus network, operated by various private companies, connects towns and villages within each district. These buses are typically older school buses or minibuses, offering basic amenities and frequent stops. Local bus fares are relatively inexpensive, making them a cost-effective choice for short-distance travel.

Express Bus Services:

For longer distances, express bus services provide a faster and more comfortable option. These buses are newer and equipped with air conditioning, reclining seats, and onboard restrooms. Express bus fares are slightly higher than local bus fares, but they offer a more enjoyable travel experience for longer journeys.

Coach Services:

For those seeking a premium travel experience, coach services offer the highest level of comfort and convenience. These modern coaches are equipped with plush seating, ample legroom, air conditioning, onboard restrooms, and sometimes even Wi-Fi connectivity. Coach fares are the highest among all bus options, but they provide a luxurious and relaxing travel experience.

Popular Bus Routes:

Some of the most popular bus routes in Belize include:

- Belize City to San Ignacio: Connecting the country's largest city with the cultural hub of Western Belize.

- Belize City to Belmopan: Traveling from the capital city to the nation's capital.

- Belize City to Dangriga: Linking the coastal city with the Garifuna community in southern Belize.

- Belize City to Placencia: Providing access to the popular beach destination in southern Belize.

- Belize City to Punta Gorda: Connecting the northern coastal city with the southernmost town in Belize.

Booking Bus Tickets:

Bus tickets can be purchased directly from bus terminals, at ticket offices, or through online booking platforms. It's advisable to book tickets in advance, especially during peak season, to secure your seat and avoid queues.

Luggage Allowance:

Bus companies typically allow one checked bag weighing up to 50 lbs (23 kg) and one carry-on bag weighing up to 10 lbs (4.5 kg). Additional baggage fees may apply for exceeding the allowance.

Travel Documents:

For domestic bus travel within Belize, passengers only need to present a valid government-issued photo ID.

- Arrive early at bus terminals to ensure ample time for boarding and ticket purchases.

- Keep your valuables secure during the journey.

- Allow extra time for transfers and potential delays.

- Enjoy the scenery and interactions with fellow passengers.

Belize's bus and coach services offer a convenient, affordable, and authentic way to experience the country's diverse landscapes, cultures, and communities. As you embark on your journey, embrace the local flavor and immerse yourself in the vibrant tapestry of Belize.

Rental Cars

Renting a car in Belize is an excellent option for those who want the freedom and flexibility to explore the country at their own pace. With a wide range of rental car options available, from budget-friendly economy cars to rugged SUVs for off-road adventures, you'll find the perfect vehicle to suit your needs.

Rental Car Companies:

Numerous rental car companies operate in Belize, offering services at major airports, cities, and tourist destinations. Some popular rental car companies include:

- Crystal Auto Rental

- Hertz

- AQ Belize Car Rental

- Alamo

- Enterprise Rent-A-Car

Rental Car Requirements:

To rent a car in Belize, you typically need to meet the following requirements:

- Minimum age of 21 (some companies may require 25)

- Valid driver's license from your home country (an international driver's license is recommended)

- Valid passport

- Major credit card (some companies may accept debit cards with a hold)

Rental Car Insurance:

Rental car companies offer various insurance options, including basic liability insurance, collision damage waiver (CDW), and theft protection. It's important to understand the coverage provided by each option and choose the one that best suits your needs.

Driving Conditions:

Roads in Belize vary from well-maintained highways to rugged dirt roads. Be prepared for potholes, uneven surfaces, and occasional livestock on the road. Driving in rural areas may require more caution and slower speeds.

Traffic Rules:

Traffic in Belize drives on the right side of the road. The speed limit in urban areas is generally 25 mph, and 50 mph on highways. Seatbelts are mandatory for all passengers.

Fuel Costs:

Fuel prices in Belize are comparable to those in the United States. Gas stations are available in major towns and along major highways.

Tips for Renting a Car in Belize:

- Book your car in advance, especially during peak season, to secure your desired vehicle and avoid last-minute availability issues.

- Carefully inspect the rental car for any existing damage and note it on the rental agreement.

- Understand the insurance coverage given and consider adding extra coverage if necessary.

- Drive cautiously and be aware of local traffic rules and conditions.

- Keep your rental car clean and avoid driving on restricted roads.

- • Return the vehicle in good condition and on schedule.

Renting a car in Belize provides a convenient and flexible way to explore the country's diverse landscapes, from ancient Mayan ruins to stunning beaches and lush rainforests. Embrace the freedom of the open road and create unforgettable memories on your Belizean adventure.

Taxis and Ferries

Taxis

Taxis are readily available in Belize's major cities, towns, and tourist destinations. They offer a convenient and affordable way to get around, especially for short-distance trips. Taxi fares are typically based on a zone system, with additional charges for luggage and nighttime travel. It's advisable to agree on the fare with the taxi driver before beginning your journey.

Popular Taxi Services:

- Belize City: Belize City Taxi Association

- San Ignacio: San Ignacio Taxi Association

- Ambergris Caye: San Pedro Belize Express Taxi

- Caye Caulker: Caye Caulker Water Taxi

Ferry Services:

Ferries play a crucial role in connecting Belize's mainland with its numerous islands and cayes. Various ferry companies operate regular services between major destinations, offering both passenger and vehicle transportation. Ferry schedules and fares vary depending on the route and ferry company.

Popular Ferry Routes:

- Belize City to San Pedro, Ambergris Caye

- Belize City to Caye Caulker

- Belize City to Dangriga

- Belize City to Hopkins

- Belize City to Placencia

Tips for Utilizing Taxis and Ferries:

- For taxis, agree on the fare beforehand to avoid misunderstandings.

- Consider sharing a taxi with other passengers to reduce costs.

- Book ferry tickets in advance, especially during peak season, to secure your desired departure time.

- Arrive early at ferry terminals to allow ample time for boarding and luggage check-in.

- Enjoy the scenic ferry rides and observe the marine life along the way.

Taxis and ferries offer valuable transportation options for exploring Belize's diverse landscapes and coastal destinations. They provide convenient and accessible connections, enabling you to discover the country's rich cultural heritage and natural beauty. Embrace the local flavor and immerse yourself in the vibrant experiences that Belize has to offer.

Must-Visit Destinations in Belize

Belize, a land of pristine beauty and rich cultural heritage, beckons travelers with an array of captivating destinations. Whether you're seeking azure waters teeming with marine life, lush jungles hiding ancient secrets, or vibrant cultural experiences, Belize has it all. Here are some must-see locations that should be on the agenda of every traveler:

Ambergris Caye

Ambergris Caye is Belize's largest island, renowned for its stunning turquoise waters, thriving marine life, and laid-back Caribbean atmosphere. With its vibrant coral reefs, diverse marine ecosystems, and captivating underwater scenery, it's a haven for snorkelers, divers, and beach enthusiasts. San Pedro, the main town on the island, offers a mix of local culture, delicious cuisine, and a range of accommodations to suit various preferences and budgets.

Location: Ambergris Caye is situated off the northeastern coast of Belize in the Caribbean Sea. Accessible primarily by boat or air, it's approximately 35 kilometers (22 miles) long and lies just northeast of Belize City.

Must-Knows for Visitors:

1. **Water Activities:** Ambergris Caye boasts some of the best snorkeling and diving spots in the world. Explore the Hol Chan Marine Reserve and Shark Ray Alley to swim among colorful fish, nurse sharks, and stingrays.

2. **Golf Cart Transportation:** Cars are limited on the island, and golf carts are a popular mode of transportation. Renting a cart offers a fun and convenient way to explore the island and its scenic spots.

3. **Cuisine and Nightlife:** San Pedro town offers a diverse range of dining options, from street food stalls serving local delicacies to upscale beachfront restaurants. At night, explore the vibrant nightlife scene with beach bars and live music.

4. **Barrier Reef Exploration:** The Belize Barrier Reef, a UNESCO World Heritage Site, runs parallel to Ambergris Caye. Consider taking boat tours or catamaran trips to witness the beauty of this majestic reef system.

5. **Weather:** Belize experiences a tropical climate. November to April is the dry season, perfect for outdoor activities. May to October sees more rainfall, but the temperatures remain warm.

6. **Responsible Tourism:** Respect the local environment and marine life. Avoid touching or disturbing coral reefs, and adhere to eco-friendly practices during water activities.

Caye Caulker, Belize

Caye Caulker, a charming and laid-back island, offers a slower pace compared to its neighboring Ambergris Caye. Known for its stunning azure waters, breathtaking sunsets, and a genuinely relaxed atmosphere, Caye Caulker is perfect for travelers seeking a peaceful getaway. This smaller island, divided by a narrow channel known as "The Split," exudes a quaint village vibe with colorful wooden houses, sandy streets, and a friendly local community.

Location: Caye Caulker is located northeast of Belize City, just a short boat ride away. It's a small limestone coral island that measures approximately 8 kilometers (5 miles) in length.

Must-Knows for Visitors:

1. **Laid-back Lifestyle:** Caye Caulker embodies a "go-slow" mentality. Embrace the island's relaxed vibe, where time seems to move a little slower. Enjoy lazy days lounging on the beaches or swinging in hammocks.

2. **Snorkeling and Diving:** Explore the island's vibrant marine life through snorkeling or diving tours. The Hol Chan Marine Reserve and Shark Ray Alley are easily accessible and offer fantastic underwater experiences.

3. **Fresh Seafood and Cuisine:** Indulge in fresh seafood, including lobster and conch, at local eateries and beachfront restaurants. Don't miss trying the traditional Belizean dish, "rice and beans."

4. **The Split:** Visit The Split, a popular spot for swimming, sunbathing, and enjoying stunning views. You can also find lively bars and restaurants offering refreshing drinks and local cuisine.

5. **Local Culture:** Engage with the friendly locals, learn about the Garifuna and Maya cultures, and immerse yourself in the island's unique atmosphere.

6. **Eco-Friendly Practices:** Like many areas in Belize, Caye Caulker emphasizes eco-friendly tourism. Respect the environment and marine life while participating in water activities.

Belize Barrier Reef

The Belize Barrier Reef is a magnificent natural wonder, stretching over 300 kilometers (190 miles) along the coast of Belize. As the second-largest barrier reef system globally and a UNESCO World Heritage Site, it's a haven for biodiversity and marine life. The reef is home to diverse coral formations, colorful fish species, sea turtles, rays, and countless other marine creatures.

Location: Running parallel to the Belizean coast, the Belize Barrier Reef is easily accessible from various coastal points, including popular islands like Ambergris Caye and Caye Caulker.

Must-Knows for Visitors:

1. **Diving and Snorkeling Paradise:** The reef offers unparalleled opportunities for diving and snorkeling. Explore remarkable sites such as the Great Blue Hole, Turneffe Atoll, and Lighthouse Reef Atoll.

2. **Conservation Efforts:** Support conservation efforts by adhering to eco-friendly practices, such as using reef-safe sunscreen and avoiding touching or damaging coral reefs.

3. **Marine Reserves and Protected Areas:** Discover marine reserves like Hol Chan Marine Reserve and South Water Caye Marine Reserve, which showcase the reef's extraordinary biodiversity.

4. **Guided Tours and Excursions:** Numerous tour operators offer guided trips, allowing visitors to witness the reef's beauty and learn about its significance from knowledgeable guides.

5. **Weather Considerations:** Plan visits during the dry season (November to April) for optimal visibility and ideal water conditions for underwater activities.

San Ignacio

San Ignacio, the lively town located in the picturesque Cayo District, offers a blend of cultural richness, adventure, and natural beauty. The Cayo District is renowned for its diverse landscapes, ranging from lush rainforests to majestic Maya ruins, providing a unique experience for travelers seeking both exploration and immersion in local culture.

Location: San Ignacio is situated in western Belize, serving as the gateway to the Cayo District. It's approximately 130 kilometers (80 miles) west of Belize City.

Must-Knows for Visitors:

1. **Maya Ruins and Archaeological Sites:** Explore ancient Maya ruins like Xunantunich, Cahal Pech, and Caracol, offering fascinating insights into Belize's rich history and civilization. The impressive structures amidst the jungle backdrop make for an awe-inspiring visit.

2. **Actun Tunichil Muknal (ATM) Cave:** Embark on an adventure to the ATM Cave, an underground realm revealing ceremonial artifacts and skeletal remains. This cave exploration provides an unforgettable and immersive experience into Maya history and spirituality.

3. **Nature and Adventure:** Engage in various outdoor activities such as cave tubing along river systems, zip-lining through the rainforest canopy, or exploring the Mountain Pine Ridge Forest Reserve with its waterfalls and natural pools.

4. **Local Markets and Cuisine:** Wander through San Ignacio's vibrant marketplaces, offering a glimpse into local life. Sample traditional Belizean dishes like rice and beans, stewed chicken, and fry jacks at local eateries and food stalls.

5. **River Tours and Wildlife:** Take River tours along the Macal and Mopan rivers, observing diverse wildlife such as howler monkeys, colorful birds, and iguanas amidst the lush jungle backdrop.

6. **Respectful Tourism:** Respect the cultural sites, local communities, and natural environment by adhering to responsible tourism practices and leaving minimal impact.

Placencia

Placencia, a slender peninsula bordered by the Caribbean Sea on one side and a lagoon on the other, is a laid-back paradise known for its pristine beaches, vibrant culture, and a relaxed atmosphere. This charming destination offers a mix of tranquility and adventure, making it a sought-after destination for travelers seeking sun-soaked relaxation and exciting experiences.

Location: Placencia Peninsula is located in southern Belize, approximately 140 kilometers (87 miles) south of Belize City.

Must-Knows for Visitors:

1. **Beaches and Water Activities:** Enjoy miles of powdery white sand beaches ideal for sunbathing, swimming, and beachcombing. Placencia offers fantastic opportunities for snorkeling, diving, fishing, and kayaking in the crystal-clear waters.

2. **Placencia Village:** Explore the colorful Placencia Village, known for its lively local art scene, eclectic shops, and charming cafes serving freshly caught seafood and local cuisine.

3. **Laughing Bird Caye National Park:** Discover the nearby Laughing Bird Caye National Park, a protected marine reserve offering remarkable snorkeling spots amid stunning coral formations and diverse marine life.

4. **Cultural Immersion:** Engage with the Garifuna culture through music, dance, and traditional cuisine. Don't miss the chance to experience the unique rhythms of Punta music and savor Hudut, a traditional Garifuna dish.

5. **Island Hopping and Excursions:** Take day trips to nearby cayes (small islands), such as Ranguana Caye or Silk Caye, for a secluded and picturesque island experience.

6. **Nature Reserves and Wildlife:** Explore nearby nature reserves like Cockscomb Basin Wildlife Sanctuary, home to jaguars and other exotic wildlife, or Monkey River, where boat tours offer sightings of manatees and howler monkeys.

Hopkins

Hopkins, a quaint coastal Garifuna village, exudes a laid-back ambiance and rich cultural heritage. Situated amidst a backdrop of verdant forests and sandy beaches, Hopkins offers an authentic and immersive experience, providing a glimpse into traditional Garifuna life and warm hospitality.

Location: Hopkins is located in southeastern Belize, approximately 130 kilometers (81 miles) south of Belize City.

Must-Knows for Visitors:

1. **Garifuna Culture:** Immerse yourself in the vibrant Garifuna culture through drumming, dancing, and traditional rituals. Visit the Lebeha Drumming Center or take part in a drumming lesson to experience the unique rhythms.

2. **Beach and Water Activities:** Enjoy long stretches of unspoiled beaches ideal for swimming, sunbathing, and beachfront relaxation. Hopkins offers snorkeling, kayaking, and fishing excursions in the nearby waters.

3. **Local Cuisine:** Delight in Garifuna cuisine, featuring delectable dishes like hudut (coconut fish stew), cassava bread, and delicious seafood served at local restaurants and eateries.

4. **Cockscomb Basin Wildlife Sanctuary:** Take a day trip to the nearby Cockscomb Basin Wildlife Sanctuary to explore hiking trails, observe diverse bird species, and potentially spot jaguars in their natural habitat.

5. **Community Tours and Workshops:** Engage in community tours, cultural workshops, and art classes to learn about traditional crafts, cooking methods, and the unique history of the Garifuna people.

6. **Respectful Cultural Interaction:** Embrace the local customs, support community initiatives, and approach cultural experiences with respect and openness.

Lamanai

Lamanai, an ancient Maya city nestled amidst lush jungle and perched along the New River Lagoon, is a captivating archaeological site in Belize. Renowned for its impressive temples, rich history, and natural surroundings, Lamanai offers a unique glimpse into the ancient Maya civilization amid a picturesque setting.

Location: Lamanai is situated in northern Belize, near Orange Walk Town, accessible via a scenic boat ride up the New River or by road.

Must-Knows for Visitors:

1. **Maya Ruins and Architecture:** Explore the well-preserved ruins, including the High Temple, Mask Temple, and Jaguar Temple, showcasing intricate stone carvings and panoramic views from atop the temples.

2. **Wildlife and Nature:** Witness abundant wildlife during the journey to Lamanai, with opportunities to spot howler monkeys, exotic birds, and crocodiles along the New River. The site itself is surrounded by lush rainforest, adding to the natural allure.

3. **Cultural Significance:** Learn about the historical and cultural significance of Lamanai from knowledgeable guides, gaining insights into the ancient Maya civilization and its architectural achievements.

4. **Boat Tours and Excursions:** Enjoy a scenic boat tour along the New River to reach Lamanai, immersing yourself in the beauty of Belizean landscapes and observing wildlife along the way.

5. **Photography and Exploration:** Capture stunning photographs of the archaeological site amidst the jungle backdrop and enjoy exploring the various structures and plazas within Lamanai's complex.

6. **Respectful Visitation:** Respect the site's heritage by following guidelines, refraining from touching or climbing on the ruins, and preserving the area's natural and cultural integrity.

Blue Hole National Park

Blue Hole National Park, nestled within the Stann Creek District, is a natural wonder encompassing the renowned inland sinkhole known as the Blue Hole. This park showcases a diverse ecosystem of tropical forests, rivers, caves, and the iconic Blue Hole, attracting nature enthusiasts and adventurers alike.

Location: Blue Hole National Park is located in the central part of Belize, approximately 12 kilometers (7.5 miles) southeast of Belmopan, the country's capital.

Must-Knows for Visitors:

1. **Blue Hole:** Marvel at the Blue Hole, a collapsed karst sinkhole filled with crystal-clear blue waters, offering opportunities for swimming, refreshing dips, and scenic views.

2. **Hiking Trails and Nature Exploration:** Explore hiking trails that wind through the park's diverse landscapes, allowing visitors to witness diverse flora, fauna, and limestone formations.

3. **St. Herman's Cave:** Visit St. Herman's Cave, a limestone cave system within the park, offering guided tours for spelunking enthusiasts and opportunities to witness stunning cave formations.

4. **Birdwatching and Wildlife:** Discover a variety of bird species and wildlife while hiking through the park, including toucans, parrots, and howler monkeys among the lush vegetation.

5. **Educational Centers:** Visit the park's educational centers to learn about the local ecology, geology, and the importance of conservation efforts within the park.

6. **Responsible Exploration:** Respect the park's natural beauty by adhering to designated trails, leaving no trace, and supporting conservation initiatives.

Cockscomb Basin Wildlife Sanctuary

Cockscomb Basin Wildlife Sanctuary, also known as "Jaguar Preserve," is a sprawling nature reserve that stands as a testament to Belize's commitment to conservation. It encompasses a vast expanse of tropical rainforest, river systems, and diverse ecosystems, offering visitors a chance to explore pristine wilderness and witness an array of wildlife.

Location: Cockscomb Basin Wildlife Sanctuary is situated in southeastern Belize, approximately 30 kilometers (19 miles) west of the coastal town of Placencia.

Must-Knows for Visitors:

1. **Jungle Hiking Trails:** Explore a network of well-maintained hiking trails that wind through the lush rainforest, providing opportunities to observe diverse flora and fauna. Look out for jaguars, pumas, tapirs, and a myriad of bird species.

2. **Tiger Fern Waterfall:** Trek to the stunning Tiger Fern Waterfall, a highlight within the sanctuary, where visitors can swim in refreshing pools amidst the jungle surroundings.

3. **River Tubing and Swimming:** Enjoy tubing or swimming in the park's river systems, immersing yourself in the serene natural setting and enjoying the cool waters.

4. **Visitor Center and Education:** Visit the visitor center to learn about the sanctuary's conservation efforts, local wildlife, and the importance of preserving Belize's natural heritage.

5. **Birdwatching and Wildlife Observation:** Engage in birdwatching activities, spotting colorful toucans, parrots, and other exotic birds, as well as encountering diverse wildlife throughout the sanctuary.

6. **Responsible Ecotourism:** Embrace eco-friendly practices, such as carrying out any waste, respecting wildlife, and following designated trails to minimize environmental impact.

Cockscomb Basin Wildlife Sanctuary provides an immersive experience in Belize's natural wonders, allowing visitors to connect with pristine wilderness and diverse wildlife in a protected sanctuary setting.

Glover's Atoll

Glover's Atoll, a remote and pristine marine reserve, is an oasis of natural beauty and biodiversity situated within the Caribbean Sea. This UNESCO World Heritage Site encompasses a collection of small islands, mangrove cayes, vibrant coral reefs, and crystal-clear waters, offering unparalleled opportunities for diving, snorkeling, and marine exploration.

Location: Glover's Atoll is located approximately 45 kilometers (28 miles) off the coast of Belize, southeast of Belize City.

Must-Knows for Visitors:

1. **Diving and Snorkeling:** Dive into the mesmerizing underwater world teeming with vibrant marine life, colorful coral gardens, and unique reef formations. Explore dive sites like the famous "Glover's Reef Wall" and "The Aquarium."

2. **Kayaking and Paddleboarding:** Embrace the tranquility of the atoll by kayaking or paddleboarding through its calm lagoons, observing the diverse marine ecosystem from above the water.

3. **Island Camping and Beach Relaxation:** Experience secluded island camping on designated cayes within the atoll, allowing for a unique and immersive overnight stay. Enjoy serene beaches and breathtaking sunsets.

4. **Fishing and Marine Conservation:** Participate in responsible fishing excursions and learn about the marine conservation efforts aimed at preserving the delicate ecosystem of Glover's Atoll.

5. **Eco-Tourism and Sustainability:** Respect the natural environment by adhering to sustainable tourism practices, supporting conservation efforts, and leaving no trace during visits.

Glover's Atoll stands as a haven for marine enthusiasts and adventurers seeking unparalleled diving experiences, serene island escapades, and a deep appreciation for the preservation of Belize's marine ecosystems.

Outdoor Adventures

Snorkeling and Diving

Snorkeling and diving in Belize offer unparalleled opportunities to explore the vibrant marine life, spectacular coral reefs, and underwater wonders of the Caribbean Sea. Here's a guide to these exhilarating outdoor adventures:

Snorkeling and Diving in Belize

Belize is a haven for snorkeling and diving enthusiasts, boasting an extensive barrier reef system, pristine waters, and an abundance of marine biodiversity. Whether you're a novice or an experienced diver, the diverse underwater landscapes and rich aquatic life make Belize an ideal destination for these water-based activities.

Locations:

1. **Belize Barrier Reef:** The Belize Barrier Reef, a UNESCO World Heritage Site and the second-largest coral reef system globally, spans the length of Belize's coastline. It comprises various dive sites, including the iconic Blue Hole, Turneffe Atoll, and Lighthouse Reef.

2. **Caye Caulker and Ambergris Caye:** These islands serve as gateways to some of the country's best snorkeling and diving spots, offering easy access to the Belize Barrier Reef and popular sites like Hol Chan Marine Reserve and Shark Ray Alley.

3. **Glover's Atoll and Southern Cayes:** Remote atolls and southern cayes, such as Glover's Atoll and Laughing Bird Caye, provide secluded and breathtaking underwater experiences amid pristine coral formations and diverse marine life.

Must-Knows for Adventurers:

1. **Marine Life Encounters:** Dive into an underwater paradise teeming with colorful fish, nurse sharks, rays, sea turtles, and an array of coral species. Witness the vibrant marine ecosystem and explore the intricate formations of coral gardens.

2. **Diving Certification and Training:** For beginners, numerous dive shops and resorts offer certification courses and guided dives suitable for all skill levels. Experienced divers can explore deeper sites, caves, and wall dives.

3. **Snorkeling Excursions:** Snorkelers can relish in the beauty of shallow reefs, observing marine life in their natural habitats. Snorkeling tours often combine multiple sites, offering opportunities to explore diverse underwater environments.

4. **Blue Hole Expedition:** Advanced divers can embark on an awe-inspiring journey to the renowned Blue Hole, a massive underwater sinkhole boasting unique geological formations and marine encounters, including reef sharks and stalactites.

5. **Responsible Diving Practices:** Embrace responsible diving and snorkeling etiquette by respecting marine ecosystems, avoiding contact with coral, and using reef-safe sunscreen to preserve the fragile underwater environment.

Snorkeling and diving in Belize promise an unforgettable aquatic adventure, providing an up-close encounter with the diverse and mesmerizing underwater world of coral reefs, marine creatures, and captivating geological formations.

Cave Tubing in Belize

Cave tubing in Belize offers a unique and thrilling adventure, allowing explorers to float along subterranean rivers within ancient limestone caves. This outdoor activity combines natural wonder, history, and a sense of adventure in a setting shaped by thousands of years of geological formations.

Locations:

1. **Nohoch Che'en Caves Branch Archaeological Reserve:** This reserve, located near Belmopan, hosts some of the most popular cave tubing experiences in Belize. The Caves Branch River runs through extensive cave systems, offering exciting tubing adventures.

2. **Other Cave Systems:** Other notable locations for cave tubing include Barton Creek Cave and St. Herman's Cave, both offering mesmerizing experiences with their unique cave formations and historical significance.

Must-Knows for Adventurers:

1. **Guided Tours and Safety:** Cave tubing tours are typically guided experiences led by knowledgeable locals. Guides provide safety gear, including helmets, life jackets, and inner tubes, ensuring a secure and enjoyable journey.

2. **Cave Exploration:** Drift through underground caverns adorned with stalactites, stalagmites, and ancient Maya artifacts. Enjoy the surreal beauty of these natural wonders while floating along the river's gentle currents.

3. **Historical and Geological Insights:** Learn about the geological history of the caves, the Maya civilization, and the

significance of these underground formations from experienced guides during the excursion.

4. **Nature and Tranquility:** Experience the serene ambiance within the caves, surrounded by the sounds of dripping water, echoing chambers, and the mystical allure of the underground world.

5. **Physical Requirements:** Cave tubing is suitable for most ages and fitness levels, although it involves moderate physical activity. Participants should be comfortable floating on the water with occasional walking through cave passages.

Cave tubing in Belize offers an enchanting journey through ancient underground rivers and caverns, providing an adventurous and educational experience within the heart of Belize's natural wonders.

Zip-lining in Belize

Zip-lining in Belize offers an adrenaline-pumping aerial adventure, allowing thrill-seekers to soar through lush tropical canopies and experience breathtaking views of the rainforest from a unique perspective.

Locations:

1. **Belize Jungle Zip-line Tours:** Various eco-parks and adventure centers across Belize, including locations near San Ignacio, offer zip-lining experiences amidst the rainforest canopy.

2. **Mystic River Resort and Jaguar Paw:** These locations provide zip-lining opportunities combined with other adventure activities, offering an immersive rainforest experience.

Must-Knows for Adventurers:

1. **Safety and Equipment:** Zip-lining tours are conducted with safety as a priority, providing participants with harnesses, helmets, and thorough safety briefings before the adventure.

2. **Canopy Views and Thrills:** Soar through the treetops on zip lines, experiencing the rush of adrenaline as you glide between platforms and enjoy breathtaking vistas of the rainforest canopy.

3. **Eco-Tourism and Nature Observation:** Gain insights into the local flora and fauna while traversing the canopy, observing wildlife such as birds, monkeys, and tropical plants.

4. **Varied Courses:** Zip-line tours often offer multiple lines with varying heights and lengths, catering to both beginners and thrill-seekers looking for an exhilarating experience.

5. **Physical Requirements:** Participants should generally be in good health and have moderate physical capabilities for short hikes to zip-line platforms and stairs to elevated launch points.

Zip-lining in Belize provides an exhilarating adventure, combining adrenaline-pumping thrills with an immersive rainforest experience and stunning aerial views of the lush canopy.

Wildlife Watching in Belize

Belize's diverse ecosystems and protected areas make it a prime destination for wildlife enthusiasts. From vibrant birdlife to iconic mammals and marine creatures, Belize offers exceptional opportunities for observing a rich variety of species.

Locations:

1. **Cockscomb Basin Wildlife Sanctuary:** Known for its jaguar conservation efforts, this sanctuary offers opportunities to spot various wildlife species, including howler monkeys, tapirs, and numerous bird species.

2. **Crooked Tree Wildlife Sanctuary:** A haven for birdwatchers, this sanctuary is home to an array of migratory and resident bird species, especially during the dry season.

3. **Marine Reserves:** Snorkeling and diving sites along the Belize Barrier Reef offer encounters with marine wildlife such as colorful fish, sea turtles, rays, and nurse sharks.

Must-Knows for Wildlife Enthusiasts:

1. **Birdwatching Hotspots:** Explore diverse habitats like forests, wetlands, and coastal areas to observe a wide variety of bird species, including toucans, parrots, herons, and the endangered scarlet macaw.

2. **Wildlife Tours and Guides:** Join guided tours led by knowledgeable naturalists and local guides who can identify wildlife species and provide insights into their behavior and habitats.

3. **Jungle Treks and Night Safaris:** Take part in jungle hikes, night walks, or river safaris to witness nocturnal creatures like owls, bats, nightjars, and possibly elusive jaguars or pumas.

4. **Marine Encounters:** While snorkeling or diving, marvel at the diverse marine life, observing sea turtles, reef fish, eels, and other fascinating underwater creatures.

5. **Responsible Wildlife Viewing:** Respect wildlife habitats, maintain a safe distance, and avoid disturbing or feeding wild animals to ensure their well-being and natural behaviors.

Wildlife watching in Belize offers an immersive experience, allowing visitors to connect with nature and observe a rich tapestry of terrestrial and marine species within diverse ecosystems.

Birdwatching in Belize

Belize's diverse habitats, ranging from lush rainforests to coastal wetlands, make it a paradise for birdwatchers. With over 600 bird species, including migratory and resident avifauna, Belize offers exceptional opportunities for birdwatching enthusiasts.

Key Birdwatching Locations:

1. **Crooked Tree Wildlife Sanctuary:** Known as a birdwatching haven, this wetland sanctuary hosts an array of bird species,

including the iconic jabiru stork, herons, egrets, and migratory birds during the dry season.

2. **Cockscomb Basin Wildlife Sanctuary:** Explore diverse habitats within this sanctuary, spotting toucans, parrots, trogons, and the elusive scarlet macaw amidst the rainforest canopy.

3. **Blue Hole National Park:** Witness various bird species, including flycatchers, warblers, and woodpeckers, while hiking through the park's tropical forests and limestone formations.

Must-Knows for Birdwatchers:

1. **Local Guides and Tours:** Engage knowledgeable local guides or join birdwatching tours for expert insights into bird species' habits, calls, and prime viewing locations.

2. **Early Morning and Evening Observations:** Birdwatching is best during early mornings or late afternoons when bird activity is high. Quietly observe bird behavior and listen for distinct calls.

3. **Binoculars and Field Guides:** Carry binoculars, field guides, and bird identification books to enhance your birdwatching experience by observing intricate details and identifying species.

4. **Respectful Observations:** Avoid disturbing nesting birds or their habitats, maintain a safe distance, and minimize noise to ensure minimal disturbance to the birds.

Birdwatching in Belize offers an immersive and rewarding experience, allowing enthusiasts to observe a diverse array of birdlife in its natural habitats across various ecosystems.

River Kayaking and Canoeing in Belize

Belize's rivers and waterways offer fantastic opportunities for kayaking and canoeing adventures, allowing explorers to navigate through serene landscapes, observe wildlife, and immerse themselves in nature's beauty.

Popular River Routes:

1. **Macal River:** Flowing through the Cayo District, the Macal River provides picturesque scenery, offering kayakers a chance to paddle past lush rainforest and occasional wildlife sightings.

2. **Mopan River:** Adjacent to the Macal River, the Mopan River offers a similar scenic experience, passing through diverse landscapes and providing opportunities for peaceful paddling.

Must-Knows for Kayakers and Canoeists:

1. **Guided Tours and Rentals:** Join guided kayaking tours or rent kayaks/canoes from reputable operators, ensuring safety and knowledge of the river routes and conditions.

2. **Wildlife Observation:** Keep an eye out for wildlife along the riverbanks, including iguanas, tropical birds, howler monkeys, and occasional river otters or turtles.

3. **Paddling Difficulty and Duration:** Choose routes suitable for your skill level, as river currents and water levels may vary.

Plan for an appropriate duration considering the chosen route and any stops along the way.

4. **Safety Precautions:** Wear appropriate safety gear, including life jackets, and stay aware of weather conditions to ensure a safe and enjoyable paddling experience.

River kayaking and canoeing in Belize offer a peaceful and immersive way to explore the country's natural beauty, providing opportunities for wildlife observation and tranquil river experiences.

Hiking and Jungle Trekking in Belize

Belize's diverse landscapes, including lush rainforests and ancient Maya sites, offer excellent opportunities for hiking and jungle trekking adventures. These experiences lead adventurers through pristine wilderness, revealing the country's natural wonders and cultural heritage.

Popular Hiking Destinations:

1. **Cockscomb Basin Wildlife Sanctuary:** Explore well-marked hiking trails, such as the Waterfall Trail, providing opportunities to observe wildlife, discover waterfalls, and trek through tropical rainforest scenery.

2. **Maya Mountains and Mountain Pine Ridge:** Trek through the rugged terrain, visiting sites like Thousand Foot Falls and exploring diverse landscapes, including pine forests and limestone caves.

Must-Knows for Hikers and Trekkers:

1. **Trail Difficulty and Length:** Choose trails suitable for your fitness level and duration preferences, considering varying terrains, elevations, and trail lengths.

2. **Guided Tours and Safety:** Consider guided tours led by experienced guides familiar with the area's flora, fauna, and history, ensuring a safe and educational trekking experience.

3. **Ecological Awareness:** Respect nature by staying on designated trails, avoiding littering, and leaving no trace to preserve the ecosystem and protect wildlife habitats.

4. **Essential Gear and Supplies:** Carry sufficient water, snacks, appropriate footwear, insect repellent, sun protection, and a first-aid kit for a comfortable and safe hike.

Hiking and jungle trekking in Belize offer thrilling opportunities to explore diverse landscapes, encounter wildlife, and uncover the natural and cultural heritage of this stunning Central American country.

Cave Exploration in Belize

Belize's limestone terrain is riddled with fascinating caves, providing adventurers with an opportunity to explore ancient Maya ceremonial sites, stunning geological formations, and underground rivers. Cave exploration unveils a mysterious world, combining history, adventure, and natural wonder.

Key Cave Exploration Locations:

1. **Actun Tunichil Muknal (ATM) Cave:** This renowned cave hosts ancient Mayan artifacts, ceramics, and skeletal remains. Visitors can embark on a guided journey through chambers adorned with pottery and calcified skeletons.

2. **Barton Creek Cave:** Traverse this river cave by canoe, discovering ancient Maya artifacts and observing magnificent cave formations, including stalactites and stalagmites.

Must-Knows for Cave Explorers:

1. **Guided Tours and Safety:** Cave exploration often requires expert guidance due to potential hazards and the need for respecting cultural artifacts. Engage with experienced local guides who prioritize safety and historical preservation.

2. **Physical Fitness and Equipment:** Some cave tours may involve physical challenges like climbing or swimming. Proper footwear, helmets, headlamps, and safety gear are essential for an enjoyable and safe experience.

3. **Respect for Cultural Heritage:** Show respect for the historical significance of cave sites by following instructions, refraining from touching artifacts, and adhering to preservation guidelines.

4. **Ecological Sensitivity:** Preserve cave ecosystems by not disturbing formations, avoiding littering, and minimizing any impact on delicate environments.

Cave exploration in Belize offers an unforgettable journey into the depths of history and natural beauty, providing an immersive experience for adventure seekers and history enthusiasts alike.

Sailing and Kayaking in Coastal Waters of Belize

Sailing and kayaking along Belize's stunning coastline offer a blend of relaxation and adventure. With its crystal-clear waters, diverse marine life, and secluded cayes, Belize provides an ideal setting for serene sailing trips and exhilarating kayaking adventures.

Popular Coastal Waters and Cayes:

1. **Ambergris Caye and Caye Caulker:** These islands serve as gateways to coastal adventures, offering opportunities for sailing and kayaking amid vibrant coral reefs, mangroves, and turquoise waters.

2. **Glover's Atoll and Lighthouse Reef:** Explore these remote atolls by sailboat or kayak, discovering pristine beaches, coral gardens, and secluded cayes within protected marine reserves.

Must-Knows for Coastal Water Adventurers:

1. **Sailing and Catamaran Tours:** Join sailing tours or charter catamarans to explore the Belizean coast, enjoying snorkeling stops, sunset sails, and visits to uninhabited cayes.

2. **Kayaking Expeditions:** Experience guided or self-guided kayak tours, paddling through calm waters, exploring mangrove channels, and discovering secluded beaches or small cayes.

3. **Marine Encounters:** Keep an eye out for diverse marine life, including sea turtles, rays, manatees, and colorful fish species while exploring coastal waters.

4. **Weather Awareness:** Consider weather conditions and tidal patterns when planning sailing or kayaking adventures to ensure safe and enjoyable excursions.

Sailing and kayaking along Belize's coastal waters offer a serene escape and exhilarating exploration, providing an opportunity to immerse oneself in the region's natural beauty and marine diversity.

Off-Roading and ATV Tours in Belize

Off-roading and ATV tours in Belize cater to adventure enthusiasts seeking exhilarating rides through rugged terrains, exploring diverse landscapes, and experiencing the country's natural wonders from a thrilling perspective.

Key Off-Roading Locations:

1. **Mountain Pine Ridge:** Embark on ATV tours through this region, traversing pine forests, crossing rivers, and visiting attractions like waterfalls, natural pools, and scenic viewpoints.

2. **Southern Belize:** Explore off-road trails through the Southern Highway, discovering remote villages, tropical forests, and hidden natural gems in the Toledo District.

Must-Knows for Off-Road Adventurers:

1. **ATV Rentals and Tours:** Rent ATVs or join guided ATV tours provided by experienced operators, ensuring safety measures and proper equipment for off-roading adventures.

2. **Trail Difficulty and Duration:** Choose trails suitable for your skill level and interests, considering factors such as terrain, duration, and any necessary permits for accessing certain areas.

3. **Exploration and Sightseeing:** Enjoy scenic rides through diverse landscapes, stopping at viewpoints, natural landmarks, and cultural sites for a comprehensive exploration experience.

4. **Safety and Equipment:** Wear protective gear, including helmets, and adhere to safety instructions provided by tour guides for a safe and enjoyable off-road adventure.

Conclusion: Off-roading and ATV tours in Belize offer adrenaline-filled experiences, allowing adventurers to discover remote landscapes, cultural sites, and natural treasures within the country's diverse terrain.

Cultural Experiences

Belize is not only rich in natural beauty but also steeped in diverse cultural traditions. To truly immerse yourself in the country's vibrant culture, consider these unique cultural experiences:

Garifuna Drumming and Dance in Belize

Garifuna culture, deeply rooted in Belize's heritage, showcases vibrant music, dance, and traditional rituals. Engaging in Garifuna drumming and dance offers visitors an immersive experience, providing insights into the rich cultural tapestry of Belize.

Cultural Centers and Performance Locations:

1. **Dangriga and Hopkins:** These coastal communities are renowned for their preservation of Garifuna traditions, hosting cultural centers, drum schools, and performances.

2. **Punta Gorda:** Explore this southern town for authentic Garifuna experiences, including drumming circles, live music, and cultural events.

Must-Knows for Cultural Enthusiasts:

1. **Drumming Workshops:** Participate in drumming workshops conducted by experienced Garifuna musicians, learning traditional rhythms and drumming techniques that form the heartbeat of Garifuna music.

2. **Dance Performances:** Witness vibrant dance performances featuring Punta and Paranda dances, characterized by energetic movements, colorful attire, and storytelling through rhythmic motion.

3. **Cultural Immersion:** Engage with local communities, join drumming circles, and participate in dance workshops to gain firsthand experiences and a deeper understanding of Garifuna traditions.

4. **Culinary Delights:** Explore Garifuna cuisine, savoring dishes like Hudut (coconut fish stew), Cassava Bread, and Ereba (cassava pancakes), often accompanied by local music and dance.

5. **Respect for Culture:** Embrace Garifuna traditions with respect, showing appreciation for their heritage, customs, and the significance of music and dance in preserving cultural identity.

Participating in Garifuna drumming and dance offers an immersive cultural journey, allowing visitors to connect with the rhythms, movements, and traditions deeply rooted in Belizean history and heritage.

Mayan Ruins Exploration

Belize is home to an impressive array of ancient Maya ruins, offering travelers a glimpse into the rich history and culture of this powerful civilization. From exploring the sprawling metropolis of Caracol, the largest ancient Maya city in Belize, to ascending the towering temples of Xunantunich, visitors can delve into the mysteries of the Maya and uncover their profound connection to the natural world.

Must-Visit Mayan Ruins:

1. Caracol: Nestled deep within the Belizean jungle, Caracol boasts the tallest man-made structure in Belize, the Sky Temple, offering panoramic views of the surrounding landscape. Explore the intricate plazas, ball courts, and

temples, and imagine the bustling life of this once-thriving metropolis.

2. Xunantunich: Perched atop a hill overlooking the Belize River, Xunantunich offers a captivating blend of natural beauty and ancient grandeur. Ascend the El Castillo pyramid, the second-tallest structure in Belize, and revel in the panoramic views. Discover the enigmatic Group A complex, adorned with intricate carvings and sculptures.

3. Lamanai Archaeological Reserve: Surrounded by lush rainforests, Lamanai is a captivating Mayan site known for its unique mask temples and impressive ball courts. Explore the ceremonial center, including the Mask Temple, the Jaguar Temple, and the High Temple. Embark on a boat tour along the New River, home to crocodiles and manatees.

4. Cahal Pech: Offering a more tranquil atmosphere, Cahal Pech is a smaller but equally fascinating Maya site. Wander through the plazas, ball courts, and temples, and admire the intricate carvings and sculptures. Climb to the top of the pyramid for stunning views of the surrounding countryside.

5. Tikal National Park (Guatemala): Just across the border in Guatemala, Tikal National Park is a UNESCO World Heritage Site and one of the largest Maya cities ever discovered. Explore the breathtaking Grand Plaza, the towering Temple I, and the Temple II, and immerse yourself in the sheer scale and grandeur of this ancient metropolis.

The Belize Barrier Reef

The Belize Barrier Reef, the world's second-largest barrier reef system after the Great Barrier Reef of Australia, is a captivating underwater wonderland teeming with marine life and vibrant coral reefs. Stretching along the Belizean coastline for over 190 miles, this UNESCO World Heritage Site offers a mesmerizing spectacle of diverse marine ecosystems, from colorful coral formations to an abundance of sharks, fish, turtles, and other aquatic animals.

Unveiling the Underwater Realm:

Embark on an unforgettable snorkeling or diving adventure and explore the breathtaking depths of the Belize Barrier Reef. Glide through crystal-clear waters, marveling at the vibrant colors of coral reefs in various shapes and sizes. Encounter a diverse array of marine life, from playful dolphins and majestic sea turtles to schools of colorful fish and elusive sharks.

Must-Visit Dive Sites:

1. The Great Barrier Reef (Gladden Split): Witness the awe-inspiring spectacle of massive aggregations of whale sharks, the world's largest fish, peacefully feeding on plankton.

2. The Blue Hole: Experience the thrill of diving into this natural sinkhole, one of the most iconic dive sites in the world. Explore its depths, from the sunlit shallows to the eerie darkness of the deeper sections.

3. Shark Ray Alley: Snorkel or dive among gentle nurse sharks and majestic stingrays gliding effortlessly through the shallow waters. Observe their graceful movements and interact with these fascinating creatures.

4. Hol Chan Marine Reserve: Discover the vibrant marine life of this protected area, home to colorful coral reefs, abundant fish species, and a variety of marine invertebrates.

5. Laughing Bird Caye National Park: Explore the diverse ecosystems of this park, including pristine beaches, lush mangrove forests, and underwater wonders teeming with marine life.

Additional Activities:

1. Kayaking and canoeing: Embark on a serene paddling adventure through the mangrove forests and waterways surrounding the Belize Barrier Reef. Immerse yourself in the tranquility of nature and spot diverse wildlife along the way.

2. Sailing and boat tours: Take a leisurely sail or boat tour along the Belize Barrier Reef, soaking in the stunning coastal scenery and enjoying the refreshing sea breeze.

3. Glass-bottom boat tours: Observe the underwater world from the comfort of a glass-bottom boat, without getting wet. Witness the vibrant colors of coral reefs and diverse marine life.

4. Fishing: Experience the thrill of deep-sea fishing and catch a variety of fish species, including tuna, grouper, and snapper.

5. Wildlife encounters: Keep an eye out for dolphins, sea turtles, and manatees swimming along the coast or basking in the sun on secluded beaches.

Wildlife Reserves and Sanctuaries

Belize is home to a variety of wildlife reserves and sanctuaries that offer visitors the opportunity to see and learn about the country's diverse flora and fauna.

Below are some of the most well-liked ones:

Cockscomb Basin Wildlife Sanctuary: This 160-square-mile sanctuary is home to the endangered scarlet macaw, as well as jaguars, tapirs, and monkeys. Visitors can hike through the rainforest, go birdwatching, or take a boat tour on the Cockscomb River.

- Jaguar Reserve Nature Center: This 150-square-mile reserve is dedicated to the conservation of jaguars. Visitors can learn about these elusive cats through exhibits and presentations, and there are also opportunities to go hiking and birdwatching.

- Crooked Tree Wildlife Sanctuary: This 50,000-acre sanctuary is home to a variety of birds, including storks, parrots, and spoonbills. Visitors can take a boat tour through the wetlands, go hiking, or visit the sanctuary's museum.

- Monkey Bay Wildlife Sanctuary: This 1,000-acre sanctuary is home to a variety of monkeys, including howler monkeys, spider monkeys, and white-faced monkeys. Visitors can go hiking, birdwatching, or take a boat tour on the Belize River.

- Belize Raptor Center: This center is home to a variety of rescued raptors, including hawks, owls, and falcons. Visitors can learn about these birds through exhibits and presentations, and there are also opportunities to see them up close.

These are just a few of the many wildlife reserves and sanctuaries in Belize. With so much to see and do, Belize is a great destination for wildlife enthusiasts.

Chocolate-Making Workshops in Belize

Belize has a rich history with cacao cultivation, and chocolate-making workshops offer an immersive experience, allowing visitors to learn about the art of making chocolate, from harvesting cacao beans to crafting delicious treats.

Cacao Plantations and Chocolate-Making Locations:

1. **Toledo District:** Explore cacao farms and chocolate-making centers in this region, known for its cacao production and opportunities to participate in hands-on workshops.

2. **San Pedro and Ambergris Caye:** Discover chocolate-making experiences offered by local artisans and boutique chocolatiers, combining education with delectable tastings.

Must-Knows for Chocolate Enthusiasts:

1. **Cacao Farm Tours:** Engage in guided tours of cacao plantations, learning about the cultivation process, harvesting techniques, and the significance of cacao in Belizean culture.

2. **Chocolate-Making Workshops:** Participate in interactive workshops where you'll roast, grind, and temper cacao beans to create your own chocolate bars, truffles, or traditional Mayan beverages like hot chocolate.

3. **Tasting and Pairing Sessions:** Indulge in chocolate tastings, exploring the nuances of different cacao varieties and discovering the art of pairing chocolates with spices, fruits, or local Belizean ingredients.

4. **Cultural Significance:** Understand the historical and cultural importance of cacao to the Maya civilization and its role in

modern-day Belizean traditions through engaging narratives shared during workshops.

5. **Sustainable Practices:** Gain insights into sustainable and ethical cacao farming practices, emphasizing the importance of supporting local farmers and preserving biodiversity.

Participating in chocolate-making workshops in Belize offers a delightful and educational experience, immersing visitors in the fascinating world of cacao cultivation and chocolate production.

Cooking Classes in Belize

Cooking classes in Belize provide an opportunity to delve into the country's diverse culinary heritage, learning traditional recipes, and culinary techniques passed down through generations.

Culinary Centers and Cultural Hubs:

1. **Belize City:** Explore cooking classes offered in Belize City, where a blend of cultural influences provides a diverse culinary experience showcasing flavors from across Belize.

2. **San Ignacio and Surrounding Areas:** Discover cooking classes conducted by local chefs and culinary experts, featuring traditional Belizean dishes and techniques.

Must-Knows for Culinary Enthusiasts:

1. **Local Ingredients and Dishes:** Learn to prepare authentic Belizean dishes, such as stew chicken, rice and beans, fry jacks, ceviche, and traditional Mayan-inspired meals using fresh local produce and spices.

2. **Hands-On Experience:** Participate in hands-on cooking sessions, mastering cooking techniques, and gaining insights into the fusion of flavors that define Belizean cuisine.

3. **Cultural Context:** Understand the cultural significance of various dishes and the historical influences that have shaped Belizean culinary traditions, including Maya, Creole, Garifuna, and Mestizo influences.

4. **Cooking Demonstrations and Tastings:** Witness cooking demonstrations by skilled chefs, followed by tastings that allow you to savor the dishes prepared during the class.

5. **Celebration of Food:** Embrace the communal aspect of food in Belizean culture, appreciating the importance of sharing meals and the role of food in celebrations and gatherings.

Cooking classes in Belize provide an interactive and flavorful experience, allowing participants to immerse themselves in the country's diverse culinary heritage while mastering the art of preparing traditional Belizean dishes.

Local Festivals and Celebrations in Belize

Belize's cultural calendar is filled with vibrant festivals and celebrations that reflect the country's diverse heritage, lively traditions, and spirited community gatherings. Participating in these events offers an immersive cultural experience and a chance to celebrate alongside locals.

Key Festivals and Celebrations:

1. **September Celebrations:** Held throughout September, these festivities commemorate Belize's independence, featuring

parades, carnivals, live music, street dances, and cultural exhibitions.

2. **Garifuna Settlement Day:** Celebrated on November 19th, this event honors the arrival of the Garifuna people in Belize with vibrant drumming, traditional dances (such as Punta), reenactments, and ceremonies in towns like Dangriga and Hopkins.

3. **Dia de los Muertos (Day of the Dead):** Observe this Mexican tradition, celebrated in San Pedro and other communities with colorful altars, processions, music, and food offerings to honor departed loved ones.

4. **Carnival:** Experience Belize's version of Carnival, featuring colorful costumes, parades, music, and dance competitions in different towns, particularly in Belize City and Orange Walk.

Must-Knows for Festival Attendees:

1. **Cultural Displays:** Immerse yourself in Belizean culture by witnessing traditional dances, live music performances, drumming, and rituals that showcase the country's diverse heritage.

2. **Local Cuisine and Crafts:** Indulge in delicious Belizean street food, traditional dishes, and explore stalls selling handmade crafts, artworks, and souvenirs during these festive events.

3. **Participatory Activities:** Engage in activities like mask-making workshops, cultural exhibitions, or even join in dance workshops to learn traditional dance moves.

4. **Respectful Participation:** Respect local customs and traditions by observing and participating respectfully in the

festivities, while embracing the warm and inclusive spirit of the celebrations.

Attending local festivals and celebrations in Belize provides an opportunity to immerse oneself in the country's rich cultural tapestry, celebrating traditions, music, dance, and the vibrant spirit of the Belizean people.

Belizean Art and Craft Workshops

Belizean art and craft workshops offer a creative exploration of the country's artistic traditions, allowing participants to learn various traditional techniques and create their own unique artworks.

Artistic Hubs and Craft Centers:

1. **Belmopan and San Ignacio:** These towns host art workshops, featuring local artists and artisans who conduct classes and share their expertise in various artistic mediums.

2. **Maya Center Women's Group (Stann Creek District):** Engage in workshops led by local artisans focusing on traditional Maya crafts, such as weaving and pottery.

Must-Knows for Art Enthusiasts:

1. **Artistic Techniques:** Participate in workshops that teach traditional Belizean artistic techniques, including wood carving, basket weaving, painting, pottery, and traditional Maya textile arts.

2. **Local Materials and Inspirations:** Learn about the use of indigenous materials and cultural inspirations behind Belizean art forms, incorporating natural elements or motifs into your creations.

3. **Interaction with Artisans:** Interact with local artisans and artists, gaining insights into their creative processes, cultural influences, and the significance of art in Belizean society.

4. **Hands-On Experience:** Enjoy hands-on experiences, creating your own artworks under the guidance of skilled instructors, while also supporting local artisans and their craft traditions.

Traditional Belizean Dishes

Belizean cuisine is a vibrant fusion of Maya, Creole, and Garifuna influences, offering a delectable array of flavors that tantalize the taste buds. From hearty Creole stews to fresh seafood dishes and spicy Garifuna specialties, Belizean cuisine captures the essence of the country's rich cultural heritage.

Must-Try Belizean Dishes:

1. Rice and Beans: A staple in Belizean cuisine, rice and beans is a classic dish that comes in various versions, often served with stewed chicken, pork, or seafood. Enjoy the comforting flavors of this traditional meal.

2. Fry Jacks: A popular breakfast or snack, fry jacks are deep-fried tortillas stuffed with a variety of fillings, such as refried beans, cheese, meats, or fruits. Indulge in their crispy texture and flavorful fillings.

3. Hudut: A Garifuna delicacy, hudut is a hearty stew made with fish, plantains, coconut milk, and spices. Savor the rich flavors and comforting warmth of this traditional dish.

4. Belizean Fish Stew: Featuring fresh seafood, vegetables, and a blend of spices, Belizean fish stew is a flavorful and satisfying dish. Experience the taste of the sea with this culinary delight.

5. Chicken Escabeche: A Creole specialty, chicken escabeche is a tangy and refreshing dish made with marinated chicken, onions, peppers, and lime juice. Enjoy the zesty flavors and tender chicken.

6. Coconut Shrimp: A taste of Belize's coastal cuisine, coconut shrimp is lightly battered and fried shrimp coated in a sweet and savory coconut sauce. Delight in the crispy shrimp and flavorful sauce.

7. Belizean Fruit Cake: A rich and decadent dessert, Belizean fruit cake is packed with dried fruits, nuts, and spices, soaked in rum or brandy. Savor the sweetness and complexity of this traditional delicacy.

8. Ducuo: A Garifuna staple, ducuo is a steamed doughy ball made with coconut, bananas, and other ingredients. Experience the unique texture and flavors of this traditional dish.

9. Johnny Cakes: A versatile bread, johnny cakes are slightly sweet corn cakes that can be enjoyed for breakfast, lunch, or dinner. Pair them with your favorite Belizean dishes.

10. Belizean Rum Punch: A refreshing beverage, Belizean rum punch is a blend of rum, fruit juices, spices, and sometimes coconut milk. Enjoy the tropical flavors and invigorating taste of this signature drink.

Culinary Adventures:

Explore the culinary scene of Belize by visiting local markets, sampling street food, and experiencing authentic Belizean restaurants. Engage with the friendly locals as they prepare and serve these traditional dishes, gaining insights into the cultural significance of Belizean cuisine.

Local Eateries and Restaurants

Here are some popular local eateries and restaurants in Belize, known for their authentic Belizean cuisine and flavorful dishes:

Belize City:

1. Martha's Café: A charming local favorite, Martha's Café offers a wide range of Belizean dishes, from hearty stews to fresh seafood specialties. Indulge in their signature rice and beans, fry jacks, and coconut shrimp.

2. Riverside Tavern: Situated along the Belize River, Riverside Tavern provides a scenic atmosphere and delectable Belizean cuisine. Savor their flavorful chicken escabeche, Belizean fish stew, and hudut, a Garifuna delicacy.

3. The Sahara Grill: Renowned for its grilled meats and seafood, The Sahara Grill serves up mouthwatering dishes in a casual setting. Enjoy their juicy grilled chicken, succulent shrimp skewers, and flavorful pork chops.

4. Wet Lizard: A lively spot known for its lively atmosphere and tasty food, Wet Lizard offers a mix of Belizean cuisine and international flavors. Sample their Belizean burritos, chicken wings, and conch fritters.

5. Celebrity Restaurant: A local institution since 1962, Celebrity Restaurant is a must-visit for authentic Belizean cuisine. Experience their traditional rice and beans, ducuo, and johnny cakes.

San Ignacio:

1. Erva's Restaurant: A popular spot among locals and tourists, Erva's Restaurant offers a wide variety of Belizean dishes prepared with fresh ingredients and local flavors. Savor their flavorful stews, fried fish, and johnny cakes.

2. The Gallery Cafe: A cozy café with a welcoming atmosphere, The Gallery Cafe serves up delicious Belizean cuisine and international fare. Enjoy their hearty breakfast options, refreshing salads, and savory Belizean dishes.

3. The Guava Limb Restaurant: Known for its authentic Garifuna cuisine, The Guava Limb Restaurant offers a unique dining experience. Try their flavorful hudut, ducuo, and cassava bread.

4. El Fogon Restaurant: A local favorite, El Fogon Restaurant serves up traditional Belizean dishes in a casual setting. Indulge in their rice and beans, chicken escabeche, and fresh seafood specialties.

5. Marie's Restaurant: A family-owned restaurant with a warm ambiance, Marie's Restaurant offers a taste of home-cooked Belizean cuisine. Savor their flavorful stews, baked chicken, and johnny cakes.

Placencia:

1. Driftwood Restaurant: Situated on the beach with stunning views, Driftwood Restaurant offers a romantic setting and delectable Belizean cuisine. Enjoy their fresh seafood dishes, grilled meats, and Belizean specialties.

2. The Tipsy Tuna: A vibrant spot with a lively atmosphere, The Tipsy Tuna serves up delicious Belizean cuisine and

international flavors. Sample their Belizean burritos, coconut shrimp, and conch fritters.

3. DeAngelo's Restaurant: A local favorite known for its authentic Belizean cuisine, DeAngelo's Restaurant offers a taste of home-cooked flavors. Indulge in their rice and beans, fry jacks, and ducuo.

4. The Cozy Corner Bar & Restaurant: A relaxed spot with a casual atmosphere, The Cozy Corner Bar & Restaurant serves up delicious Belizean dishes and international fare. Enjoy their hearty burgers, fresh seafood platters, and Belizean specialties.

5. The Breeze Restaurant: Offering a taste of Belizean cuisine with a modern twist, The Breeze Restaurant provides a unique dining experience. Sample their flavorful lobster dishes, grilled meats, and Belizean specialties.

These are just a few of the many local eateries and restaurants in Belize that offer authentic Belizean cuisine and flavorful dishes. With so much to choose from, you're sure to find something to satisfy your taste buds and experience the culinary delights of this vibrant country.

Street Food Delights

Belize's street food scene is a vibrant tapestry of flavors, offering a tantalizing taste of the country's diverse culinary heritage. From savory snacks to refreshing treats, street food vendors across Belize serve up authentic dishes that capture the essence of Belizean cuisine.

Here are some of the most popular and delectable street food delights in Belize:

1. Panades: These savory deep-fried turnovers are filled with a variety of ingredients, including chicken, fish, beans, or cheese. Indulge in their crispy texture and flavorful fillings.

2. Garnaches: These small fried tortillas are topped with refried beans, cheese, and onions, often with a spicy habanero pepper sauce. Enjoy their simple yet satisfying flavors.

3. Salbutes: Similar to garnaches, salbutes feature fried tortillas topped with shredded cabbage, diced tomatoes, and a tangy lime juice mixture. Savor their fresh and zesty flavors.

4. Fry Jacks: These fluffy deep-fried dough triangles are often served with refried beans, cheese, eggs, or honey. Delight in their crispy texture and versatile combinations.

5. Hudut: This traditional Garifuna dish features mashed plantains and coconut milk, creating a smooth and creamy consistency. Experience its unique flavors and comforting warmth.

6. Belizean Fruit Cakes: These rich and decadent desserts are packed with dried fruits, nuts, and spices, soaked in rum or brandy. Savor their sweetness and complexity.

7. Johnny Cakes: These slightly sweet corn cakes are versatile bread, enjoyed for breakfast, lunch, or dinner. Pair them with your favorite Belizean dishes.

8. Belizean Rum Punch: This refreshing beverage is a blend of rum, fruit juices, spices, and sometimes coconut milk. Enjoy

the tropical flavors and invigorating taste of this signature drink.

9. Fresh Fruits: Belize is home to an abundance of tropical fruits, including mangoes, papayas, pineapples, and bananas. Sample their fresh flavors and juicy goodness.

10. Ice Cream and Sorbet: Indulge in refreshing scoops of ice cream or sorbet, made with local fruits and flavors. Enjoy their cool treats on a hot Belizean day.

Exploring the street food scene is an essential part of any Belizean adventure. As you wander through bustling markets, lively plazas, and vibrant streets, keep an eye out for these delectable treats and savor the authentic flavors of Belizean cuisine.

Language and Communication

Belize is a multilingual country with a rich linguistic heritage. The official language of Belize is English, but the most widely spoken language is Belizean Creole, a creole language based on English with influences from African, Spanish, and Mayan languages. Other languages spoken in Belize include Spanish, Garifuna, and various Mayan languages.

English:

English is the language of education, government, and business in Belize. It is also widely understood and spoken by most Belizeans. If you are an English speaker, you will have no difficulty communicating with people in Belize.

Belizean Creole:

Belizean Creole is the most commonly spoken language in Belize. It is a vibrant and expressive language with a unique grammar and vocabulary. While Belizean Creole is not as widely understood as English, it is still a valuable language to learn if you want to fully experience Belizean culture.

Spanish:

Spanish is spoken by a large minority of Belizeans, particularly in the northern and western parts of the country. Spanish is also a useful language to learn if you plan to visit neighboring Guatemala or Mexico.

Garifuna:

Garifuna is a language spoken by the Garifuna people, a group of descendants of West Africans who were deported to the Caribbean in the 18th century. Garifuna is a unique language with influences from African, Spanish, and Arawak languages.

Mayan Languages:

There are several Mayan languages spoken in Belize, including Yucatec Maya, Mopan Maya, and Kekchi Maya. These languages are spoken by the Maya people, who are the indigenous inhabitants of Belize.

Communication Tips:

- If you don't speak Belizean Creole, you can still communicate with people in Belize by speaking English slowly and clearly.

- Be patient and understanding when communicating with people who don't speak English as their first language.

- Learn a few basic phrases in Belizean Creole or Spanish to show your respect for the local culture.

- Use body language and facial expressions to communicate effectively.
- Be patient and don't get disappointed if you don't comprehend everything straight away.

- Immerse yourself in the local culture and language by listening to music, watching movies, and reading books in Belizean Creole or Spanish.

Learning about the languages of Belize will enrich your travel experience and help you connect with the local people on a deeper level.

Weather and Packing Tips

Belize's weather is predominantly tropical, with warm temperatures and high humidity throughout the year. The country experiences two distinct seasons: the dry season (November to April) and the rainy season (May to October). However, even during the rainy season, rainfall is typically concentrated in short bursts, leaving plenty of time for sunshine and outdoor activities.

Dry Season (November to April):

- Temperatures: Average temperatures range from the mid-70s to mid-80s Fahrenheit (24-29°C).

- Precipitation: Low rainfall, with occasional showers or thunderstorms.

- Humidity: Lower humidity levels compared to the rainy season.

Rainy Season (May to October):

- Temperatures: Average temperatures remain similar to the dry season, with occasional hotter days.

- Precipitation: Increased rainfall, with frequent showers and thunderstorms.

- Humidity: Higher humidity levels, especially during the peak rainy months (June to September).

Packing Tips:

Regardless of the season, here are some general packing tips for Belize:

- Lightweight and breathable clothing: Pack quick-drying fabrics like cotton or linen to stay comfortable in the warm and humid weather.

- Comfortable footwear: Bring along a pair of sturdy walking shoes for exploring ruins, hiking trails, and beaches.

- Rain gear: A raincoat or poncho is essential, especially during the rainy season.

- Sunscreen and insect repellent: Protect yourself from the sun and mosquitoes with appropriate sunscreen and insect repellent.

- Swimsuit and towel: Belize boasts stunning beaches and waterways, so don't forget your swimsuit and towel.

- Hat and sunglasses: A hat and sunglasses will shield you from the sun's rays.

- Camera and other electronics: Capture your Belizean memories with a camera or smartphone. Don't forget chargers and adapters.

- First-aid kit: Keep a basic first-aid kit on hand in case of minor injuries.

- Essential medications: Pack any prescription medications you may need.

- Water bottle that may be reused: Carry a reusable bottle of water to stay hydrated.

- Small backpack: A small backpack is handy for carrying essentials while exploring.

- Daypack or hiking backpack: If you plan on hiking or backpacking, bring an appropriate backpack.

- Travel adaptor: Belize uses two-pronged electrical outlets, so bring a travel adaptor if you have three-pronged devices.

- Currency exchange: Convert your currency to Belizean dollars (BZD) for convenient transactions.

- Important documents: Keep your passport, travel insurance, and flight itinerary secure.

Cultural Etiquette

Belize is a thriving nation with a wide range of cultures. To ensure a respectful and enjoyable travel experience, here are some essential guidelines for cultural etiquette in Belize:

Greetings and Social Interactions:

- Greetings: When greeting someone, a handshake or a friendly nod is appropriate. For closer friends or acquaintances, a hug or kiss on the cheek may be customary.

- Addressing People: Use titles and surnames when addressing someone formally. For casual interactions, first names are generally acceptable.

- Personal Space: Belizeans tend to maintain a closer personal space than in some other cultures. Be mindful of this and avoid invading personal space.

- Eye Contact: Maintain eye contact during conversations as it demonstrates respect and engagement.

Communication and Conversation:

- Language: English is the official language, but Belizean Creole is widely spoken. Learning a few basic phrases in Belizean Creole shows respect for the local culture.

- Tone of Voice: Belizeans generally have a relaxed and friendly tone of voice. Avoid being overly assertive or loud.

- Sensitive Topics: Avoid discussing sensitive topics such as politics or religion unless you are invited to do so.

- Humor: Belizeans appreciate humor and enjoy a good laugh. However, be mindful of cultural references that may not be understood by everyone.

Dress and Appearance:

- Dress modestly: When visiting religious sites or cultural attractions, dress modestly and cover your shoulders and knees.

- Beach attire: Beach attire is appropriate for beaches and resorts, but cover up when venturing into towns or cities.

- Footwear: Footwear is typically removed when entering homes or certain establishments.

- Respectful Attire: Dress appropriately for the occasion and avoid overly revealing or provocative clothing.

Dining Etiquette:

- Mealtimes: Lunch is typically served around noon, and dinner is usually around 6 pm.

- Table Manners: Use basic table manners, such as chewing with your mouth closed and avoiding talking with your mouth full.

- Gratitude: Tipping is customary in Belize. A 10-15% tip is considered appropriate for good service.

- Sharing Food: Sharing food is a common practice in Belize, especially among friends and family.

- Try Local Cuisine: Sample local dishes and beverages to experience Belizean flavors and culinary traditions.

General Customs and Traditions:

- Respect for Elders: Respect for elders is highly valued in Belizean culture. Address elders with respect and deference.

- Patience: Belizeans have a laid-back approach to life. Be patient and understanding if things don't happen as quickly as you might expect.

- Bargaining: Bargaining is acceptable in local markets and when purchasing souvenirs or handicrafts.

- Respect for Nature: Belize is home to a rich biodiversity. Be mindful of the environment and refrain from polluting or endangering natural landmarks.

- Support Local Communities: Support local communities by purchasing souvenirs and handicrafts from local artisans.

Health and Safety Guidelines

Traveling to Belize offers a plethora of opportunities to explore its diverse landscapes, rich cultural heritage, and captivating wildlife. However, ensuring your health and safety during your Belizean adventure is paramount. Here are essential guidelines to safeguard your well-being and maximize your Belizean experience:

Vaccination and Health Preparations:

- Consult your healthcare provider at least 6-8 weeks before your trip to discuss necessary vaccinations and preventive measures.
- Ensure your routine vaccinations, such as tetanus, measles, mumps, and rubella, are up to date.
- Consider getting vaccinated against hepatitis A and B, typhoid, and rabies, depending on your itinerary and activities.
- Pack a first-aid kit with essential medications, including pain relievers, antihistamines, insect repellent, sunscreen, and bandages.

Mosquito Protection:

- Mosquito-borne diseases, such as dengue and Zika virus, are prevalent in Belize.
- Apply insect repellent containing DEET or picaridin to exposed skin, especially during dusk and dawn.
- Wear long-sleeved shirts, pants, and socks to minimize skin exposure, particularly in areas with high mosquito activity.
- Consider using mosquito nets or bed nets when sleeping in open-air accommodations.

Water Safety:

- Avoid drinking tap water unless it is purified or boiled.
- Stick to bottled water, sealed beverages, and freshly boiled or filtered water.
- Exercise caution when swimming in freshwater lakes or rivers due to the risk of waterborne parasites.
- Avoid contact with open wounds or cuts with contaminated water.

Sun Protection:

- Belize's tropical climate can be intense, with strong UV rays.
- Apply sunscreen with an SPF of 30 or higher to exposed skin regularly.
- Wear a wide-brimmed hat and sunglasses to protect your face and eyes.
- Seek shade during the hottest hours of the day, typically between 10 am and 4 pm.

Wildlife Encounters:

- Belize boasts a rich abundance of wildlife, including insects, reptiles, and mammals.
- Maintain a safe distance from wild animals and avoid feeding or touching them.
- Be cautious when hiking in dense vegetation or forests, as snakes may be present.
- If encountering dangerous animals, remain calm, do not make sudden movements, and back away slowly.

Personal Safety:

- Be aware of your surroundings, especially in crowded areas or at night.
- Keep your valuables secure, avoid carrying large amounts of cash, and use reputable taxis or transportation services.
- Inform your hotel or accommodation about your travel plans and return times.
- Trust your instincts and avoid potentially risky situations.

Seek Medical Attention:

- If you experience any illness or injury during your trip, seek medical attention promptly.
- Public and private healthcare facilities are available in Belize's major cities and towns.
- international travel insurance is recommended to cover medical expenses and unexpected emergencies.

Emergency Contact Information:

Keep emergency contact information handy, including the Belize Tourist Board hotline (+501-223-0101) and the Belize Emergency Medical Service (911).

ITINERARIES SUGGESTIONS

Itinerary for History and Culture Buffs:

1. Day 1: Arrive in Belize City and check into your hotel.
2. Day 2: Visit the Museum of Belize, which houses artifacts from the country's Mayan and colonial past.
3. Day 3: Take a day trip to Altun Ha, the ruins of an ancient Mayan city.
4. Day 4: Visit the Belize Zoo, which is home to over 400 animals native to Belize.
5. Day 5: Take a boat tour of the Belize Barrier Reef, the second-largest coral reef system in the world.

Itinerary for Adventure Seekers:

1. Day 1: Arrive in Belize City and check into your hotel.
2. Day 2: Go ziplining through the rainforests of Cayo District.
3. Day 3: Go cave tubing in the Barton Creek Cave.
4. Day 4: Go on a jungle hike in the Cockscomb Basin Wildlife Sanctuary.
5. Day 5: Go scuba diving or snorkeling in the Belize Barrier Reef.

Itinerary for Beach Bums:

1. Day 1: Arrive in Ambergris Caye and check into your hotel.
2. Day 2: Spend the day relaxing on the beach.
3. Day 3: Go snorkeling or diving in the Hol Chan Marine Reserve.
4. Day 4: Take a boat tour to Secret Beach, a secluded beach that is only accessible by boat.
5. Day 5: Go kayaking or stand-up paddleboarding in the Caribbean Sea.

Itinerary for Relaxation Seekers:

1. Day 1: Arrive in Placencia, a small village on the southern coast of Belize.
2. Day 2: Spend the day relaxing on the beach.
3. Day 3: Go for a massage or spa treatment at one of the many spas in Placencia.
4. Day 4: Take a boat tour to the Laughing Bird Caye National Park, a small island with beautiful beaches and a variety of wildlife.
5. Day 5: Go for a swim or a float in the Placencia Lagoon.

Itinerary for Foodies:

1. Day 1: Arrive in Belize City and check into your hotel.
2. Day 2: Take a food tour of Belize City, which will introduce you to the country's diverse cuisine.
3. Day 3: Visit the Belize Chocolate Experience, where you can learn how chocolate is made from bean to bar.
4. Day 4: Take a cooking class and learn how to make traditional Belizean dishes.
5. Day 5: Visit the Belize Farmers Market, where you can sample and purchase local produce and other goods.

These are just a few ideas to get you started. With so much to see and do in Belize, you're sure to find an itinerary that's perfect for you.

Conclusion

As you bid farewell to the enchanting shores of Belize, carrying with you a treasure trove of memories and a heart brimming with joy, allow me to extend my heartfelt gratitude for choosing my humble guidebook as your companion on this unforgettable adventure.

Together, we've traversed the sun-kissed beaches, delved into the depths of the rainforest, and unearthed the secrets of ancient Mayan ruins. We've savored the flavors of Belizean cuisine, danced to the rhythm of Garifuna drums, and embraced the warmth and hospitality of the Belizean people.

I hope this guidebook has served as a beacon, illuminating your path through Belize's enchanting landscapes and enriching your experiences with its vibrant culture and captivating history. From snorkeling amidst vibrant coral reefs to exploring ancient ruins shrouded in mystery, Belize has unveiled its wonders before you.

As you return to your daily life, carrying the echoes of Belize's laughter and the warmth of its sun in your heart, remember that the spirit of Belize lives on within you. May the memories we've created together remain etched in your mind, a reminder of the enchanting adventure we shared.

And who knows, perhaps our paths will cross again amidst the turquoise waters and lush greenery of Belize. Until then, I bid you farewell with a heartfelt "Thank you" and a warm Belizean farewell, "Wahina!"

Printed in Great Britain
by Amazon

40602839R00066